WICK TO WEMBLEY?

... on the trail of the FA Cup

Andy Ollerenshaw

First published in 2008 by Centre Circle Publishing
www.ccpub.co.uk

PO Box 2923
Eastbourne
East Sussex
BN20 8WG

Layout, design and editing: David Bauckham
Cover design: Alun Westoll and David Bauckham
Cover photograph: Paul Baden

ISBN 978-0-9560458-0-5

Printed and bound by:
Biddles Limited
24 Rollesby Road
Hardwick Industrial Estate
Kings Lynn
Norfolk
PE30 4LS

for Mum, you always knew I would

thanks

to Angela and Joe, the only ones who truly know what this means to me

to all who have attended games with me, especially to Pete whose enthusiasm from day one was infectious and to Ann whose regular supply of Jelly Babies, Liquorice Allsorts and Wine Gums kept us going

to everyone I have met along the way, for your wholehearted encouragement and support

to Alun and Gemma without whom this book would be naked and littered with spolling mistakes

to Alistair for your unconditional help and advice

and to David who gave me the belief

Publisher's Note

I first became aware of Andy Ollerenshaw in October 2007 when a new member by the name of 'andyollers' posted a message on the unofficial forum of Eastbourne Borough FC. The gist of the message was that he was looking forward to visiting Priory Lane as the latest stage in his 'Road to Wembley' blog.

Oh well, nothing new in that. Every season lots of other football fans set out to do the same, but rarely make it all the way to the Final. However, I took a look at Andy's blog anyway. Far from being the usual review of pies and programmes, it was actually well written, and above all clearly demonstrated a passion not only for the FA Cup, but for what our National Game is (or should be) all about.

By coincidence I was engaged in a little season-long project of my own: to tell the story of the football season across Sussex. Mindful of the fact that no mainstream publisher would touch such a project with a ten foot pole, I had resolved to set up my own 'publishing house', and was looking for similar worthy projects to publish. Andy's blog appeared to fit the bill perfectly... as long as he was able to make it to the FA Cup Final at Wembley. Well, as you will read in the following pages, he did indeed!

Working with Andy on this project has been, shall we say, an 'experience'; not least because he is almost as pedantic as I am... no, he is *more* pedantic than me. Nevertheless, aside from being mutual pedants we also share a passion for football, and for what we would like the so called 'National Game' to represent. We suspect we are not alone, and if you share our passion we are sure you will find much to enjoy and identify with in this book.

DAVID BAUCKHAM

Matches Covered

1. Chertsey Town v Wick

2. Sittingbourne v Chertsey Town

3. Dartford v Sittingbourne

4. Sittingbourne v Dartford

5. Dartford v Camberley Town

6. Camberley Town v Dartford

7. Bromley v Dartford

8. Eastbourne Borough v Bromley

9. Eastbourne Borough v Weymouth

10. Cambridge United v Weymouth

11. Wolverhampton Wanderers v Cambridge United

12. Watford v Wolverhampton Wanderers

13. Cardiff City v Wolverhampton Wanderers

14. Middlesbrough v Cardiff City

15. Barnsley v Cardiff City

16. Cardiff City v Portsmouth

Introduction

In January 2008 the Reading striker, Dave Kitson, ever so eloquently declared that he "didn't give two s**ts" about the FA Cup. His disregard for the competition sparked a debate amongst football fans, experts and pundits the length and breadth of the country. Is the FA Cup dead? Have the big money football competitions such as the Premier League and the UEFA Champions League pushed the once great FA Cup into a shadowy corner that people would sooner ignore? When I say Kitson's comments sparked debate that is not strictly true. It merely trawled questions back to the surface again.

Noises and rumblings had been bubbling under for some years about the FA Cup. Had the competition lost its gloss? Was the sparkle fading? Had the romance waned? Concerns peaked in 2000 when Manchester United chose not to compete in the FA Cup in preference to a money-spinning mid-season World Club Championship in Brazil. Many then predicted the end of this great competition as we knew it. And the reported demise has filled many sports column inches since.

By total coincidence, at the time Kitson was expressing his views, I had already set off on a journey of my own to explore the FA Cup. As you will read, my journey started kind of by chance. And that little bit of fate set the tone for my adventure, one that would be controlled purely by fate and fate alone. I wanted to survey the FA Cup from its source through to its final resting place at Wembley. A journey that would begin in the dying embers of a 2007 summer, continue through the wet and cold British winter and conclude in the warming spring of 2008. A full season of English FA Cup football. I hoped to get close to the clubs and the fans and find out first-hand what the FA Cup means to everyone involved.

A journey which started as a trickle of a stream only 500 yards from my

Introduction

front door, at the home of Chertsey Town FC, I knew would become a fast flowing river that would rapidly transport me through all fourteen rounds of the competition. That was the plan. A record 731 teams entered the 2007-08 FA Cup and teams from communities, villages, towns and cities across England and Wales would be setting off on the same odyssey. Hundreds of tributaries that would eventually join the main flow. I knew that my own little stream would eventually contribute to that glorious flood we are all familiar with at the turn of the year, at the Third Round Proper stage when the big names join the draw. I knew that the waters would be rapid and at times turbulent.

But what I didn't know was where this journey would take me, in which direction it would turn or how far downstream I would manage to get. I was more than happy to thumb a lift; I just had no idea where it would kick me out.

This was by no means a unique journey. It has been done before, most famously by Brian James who wrote 'From Tividale to Wembley' in 1977. There are others I know that have done this journey this season. I am certainly not the first and I know I will not be the last. But when I started this journey back in August I turned to the most powerful tool of communication known to mankind – the Internet. I became a 'blogger' and entered a new world of online diaries, blog posts, message boards and world-wide reach. My appetite for documenting my FA Cup experiences through my blog became almost ferocious as I responded to interest from readers around the globe. I wrote several posts each week. By the time it was all over, and I came to write this book, my story was already written.

This book is therefore a collection of blog posts, with a little bit of context thrown in for good measure. It was at times tempting to change some of the articles using hindsight as a reason to edit, but I have refrained. I have left the posts intact and as such reflect my own views, opinions and feelings at frozen points in time. Please fasten your buoyancy jacket and jump aboard.

The Road Starts Here ... At The End Of My Lane

This is my first ever blog, my first ever post, and I have an apology to make already. It's my title, you see. 'Wick to Wembley?' is not quite right, it is slightly misleading. But I'll come to that in a bit.

Ever since my Dad took me to my first ever FA Cup game I fell in love with the competition and I'm still in love. Don't ask me to explain why, I don't know. My wife regularly reminds me it is football, a game, nothing more, nothing less. Twenty two people chasing a pig's bladder around a field. What is there to love?

I'll watch any football game, always have, and I always will.

But the FA Cup is special. Every season I look forward to it. The small clubs in the early rounds, the First Round Proper where there is always an upset, the Third Round where the 'big' clubs join in, the excitement of the Semi-Finals and then the Final itself, steeped in history. And don't get me started on the draws. Even better when they are live! The balls in the bag, the team numbers, the anticipation, excitement and then disappointment when your team gets Darlington (away). Fantastic.

And every year I hear myself saying the same thing "You know, one year I'm going to do a road to Wembley type thing....". Every bloody year. It drives my wife mad, I'm sure it irritates the hell out of my friends; it is even starting to annoy me now.

So, just do it. You know the thing, don't you? Go and watch your local club in the Extra Preliminary Round in August. Whichever team wins, go and see them in the next round, and so on, until you arrive at the Final. Wembley. Easy. Job done.

And so here I am, and I've been to the first match:

The Road Starts Here ... At The End Of My Lane

"Football Association Challenge Cup (sponsored by e.on) Extra Preliminary Round, Chertsey Town v Wick, Tuesday 21st August 2007 Kick-Off 7.45pm".

But this was kind of by accident really. In fact, this whole adventure may never have happened at all. All the FA Cup Extra Preliminary Round games were played out over the weekend of 17th, 18th and 19th August. And I was busy. Once again, I thought I had missed my chance. Another year of saying "You know, one year I'm going to do this...".

In that first game, Chertsey Town were 2-0 down away at Wick, a small community outside Littlehampton, West Sussex. 2-0 down with six minutes to play and seemingly heading for an early exit from this season's competition. Two late goals forced a replay, a relief (no doubt) for the Chertsey Town club and their fans but no less than a twist of fate for me.

And the replay was on Tuesday night. Nothing on the TV and Chertsey Town's home ground only a stone's throw from my home. At the end of my lane, to be precise. Why not? A five minute stroll to the ground just in time to see the players run out.

But it was only on the way back from Chertsey's ground that I decided to attempt this road to Wembley venture. You could say that all this started on the back of a mere whim. A last-minute decision to pop down to a game at the end of my lane. No months and months of planning, no checking of fixture dates, no rearranging holidays and family events. None of that at all.

No late goals from Chertsey, no road to Wembley this year. No blog. Many people believe that our lives are already mapped out and fate controls our destiny. Those two late goals in Sussex may have determined my fate for the next few months and could now set me off on a course of events that I will have no control over whatsoever. The only things I can say with any degree of certainty is that I have made the decision to do a road to Wembley this season and that it started at Chertsey Town on Tuesday evening. But I have no idea where the road will take me. I have been to one game already but I have no way of knowing how many games I will end up watching or where I will be off to next. I will have no say in matters, I will have no choice. Which clubs will I visit? Which villages, towns or cities? The moment I will know is the moment the numbered balls emerge from the FA's bag. Only at that point in time will I know the next direction I will be headed and the date of my next trip. For me this season, the FA Cup draws will take on a completely different meaning. It's all a bit scary really.

And this is where my apology enters, stage left. My blog title. My first game was the replay at Chertsey Town. I didn't start at Wick, but 'Wick to Wembley' sounds a little snappier than 'Chertsey Town to Wembley'. Sorry.

But why the question mark in 'Wick to Wembley?' Well, I'm not sure if I can do it. It's a tall order. Obscure grounds in places (or even parts of the country) I've never been to before. The distances to travel. The cost. The availability of tickets in the latter rounds. My wife. My child. The inane sadness of it all.

Excuses? Who knows? In the meantime - come on in, the water is lovely.

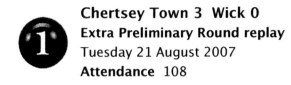

Chertsey Town 3 Wick 0
Extra Preliminary Round replay
Tuesday 21 August 2007
Attendance 108

Chertsey is a small town tucked in between the Rivers Thames and Bourne, and the motorways M3 and M25. You don't pass through Chertsey, nor end up there by mistake. You only go to Chertsey if you plan to go there; it is not a football town. The ground is hidden away in amongst the Victorian terraces, out of sight, at the foot of Alwyns Lane. The town makes no boasts about its club; it does not get any mention in the free local newspaper (that honour goes to Walton & Hersham). Its shop windows do not advertise its games. There are no pubs displaying the team colours (blue and white). The only way a stranger would know there is a football team here was if he spied the sign pointing (with hope rather than any real purpose) to the ground or if he happened to spot the photo of Chertsey Town youth team in the chippy.

Chertsey ply their trade in the Combined Counties League Premier Division and any attendance over 100 is good. I imagine their ground is typical for their football pyramid status, but I can't say as I haven't been to many games at this level. A single turnstile into the ground (£6) and (although it goes without saying) it is soon evident that there is no Abramovich or Shinawatra here to throw the big bucks around. The ground has a slightly run-down feel, flaking paint and ageing concrete.

However, the passion is there. Clubs at this level rely on the many who work tirelessly in the name of the club. And they were out in force tonight for the big Cup game. The turnstile operators, the bar staff, the ninety year old groundsman and the suited club officials.

And a reasonable crowd (108), of which (I'm guessing) four were from Wick (near Littlehampton in West Sussex).

3-0 was a fair result. Chertsey were strong on the night, solid at the back and gave Wick few sights of goal. The standard of football was good; speed and strength most important, with glimpses of skill thrown in

Game 1 Chertsey Town 3 Wick 0

for good measure. Tackles were uncompromising, it certainly wasn't a game for the faint-hearted and to prove the point Wick had a player dismissed late on for a challenge that catapulted a Chertsey winger into the crowd.

I think the locals were happy. We even had renditions of "We're all off to Wembley, we're all off to Wembley, na-na, na, na...". The romance of the Cup.

Just don't tell anyone in the town.

Draw for the <u>Preliminary Round</u>: Sittingbourne v Chertsey Town.

And so to the next round. On Saturday, 1st September and it is a trip to Sittingbourne. But where is Sittingbourne? Anyone got a map?

Holiday Season

The enormity of what I am planning to do is slowly sinking in. Call me stupid (most people do), but it takes a while for the grey matter to register. If I am to see this through, I'm talking about 14 ties in total, including the Final. The earlier rounds are regionalised, so travel shouldn't be too much of a problem. But what about the First Round Proper and onwards? Carlisle v Wrexham on a wet Saturday in November? Nuts.

But these are, surely, more excuses.

The first trip for me is to Kent. Sittingbourne sits between Maidstone and the Isle of Sheppey and the football team plays in the Ryman Isthmian League, Division One South, one level above Chertsey Town. I've never been to that part of the country, and it will be a bit of a trek (about 120 miles there and back) but I'm up for it.

In an earlier post I mentioned how introverted Chertsey is when it comes to its football team. On the eve of their tie at Sittingbourne, it's true to say that Chertsey is not sweating with an FA Cup fever. Hardly surprising, the kids aren't even back at school yet.

Today I paid good money for a copy of the local paper, the Surrey Herald. Chertsey Town did get some coverage in the back pages with reports on their last two League games (a 3-0 home win over Raynes Park Vale and a 4-1 tonking at Bedfont). But no specific preview of the Cup tie.

One thing did catch my eye though. I know that football at this level is a million miles removed from your Chelseas or Man Uniteds. But buried in the report on the Bedfont defeat, without any sense of surprise or bemusement, was the following quote about the under strength Chertsey team:

Holiday Season

"Injuries and non-availabilities had decimated the Chertsey side. Four key members of the squad were away on holiday".

Come again? On holiday?

Imagine Arsene Wenger's reaction if Theo Walcott phoned in to explain that he would miss the Sparta Prague game 'cos he had a week booked at Butlins (pretty good crèche there Theo).

But this happens in the lower Leagues. The bread and butter games are the League games against the likes of Ash United, Cove or Dorking and in many cases family commitments come first. The FA Cup is a diversion. But a welcome diversion. Up and down the length of the country this weekend, from Consett to Wootton Bassett, there will be players of all ages and experiences getting excited about playing in the FA Cup. For many, just to play in an FA Cup match will be the fulfillment of a dream.

And on this first weekend in September, numerous teams will be playing in their own Cup Final. I just hope the Chertsey lads are back from the beach in time for theirs.

Sittingbourne 1 Chertsey Town 0
Preliminary Round Saturday 1 September 2007
Attendance 194
Distance travelled 131 miles

Huge open skies.

My first visit to this part of England and the thing that struck me most is the sky. It just seemed so, well, how can I put it?

Big.

A big expanse of sky. And, taking its place below, Sittingbourne FC sitting in a big expanse of space. The Sittingbourne ground, Bourne Park, sits next to the bigger Greyhound Stadium, but both stadia are surrounded by so much open, concreted, land. Compared to the Chertsey ground, which seems to have been shoe-horned into the town, Sittingbourne's ground couldn't be any more different.

The approach towards the ground, north and east of the town, is through a business park-cum-industrial estate with wide-open, unmarked roads. The entrance to the Central Park Stadium complex is through a set of overly grand gates. You have to drive through a huge (upper) car park to get to the large (lower) car park adjacent to the Sittingbourne ground. A vast amount of space for a club which attracts between 150 and 200 supporters.

There is a reason for all this space around the ground and that is due in no small part to Sittingbourne's tumultuous history.

Sittingbourne FC were born in 1881 and were called Sittingbourne United for the first five years of their life before the 'United' part of their name was dropped. In 1888 they merged with another local club (oddly named 'Nil Desperandums'). In 1892 the club moved to a meadow behind the Bull Hotel and this became their ground right up to 1989.

Sittingbourne went through a couple of financially difficult periods

Game 2 Sittingbourne 1 Chertsey Town 0

before and after the Second World War, but these were nothing in comparison to the almost disastrous money problems experienced by the Kent outfit in the 1990s.

Problems started in 1990 when the club sold their Bull ground (they had bought the ground back in 1954 with help from the FA and club supporters) for a whopping £4.5 million. With the money received, Sittingbourne had ambitious plans and gambled on success on the pitch, something that many League clubs have done in recent years and ultimately regretted. Leeds United spring to mind. Sittingbourne purchased a 23 acre site on a Eurolink estate and built a 2000 seat stand which was the centrepiece of the new Central Park stadium. By 1994 Greyhound Racing had also been introduced. At the peak of their success they were promoted (1992-93) to the Beazer Home League Premier Division and were attracting large gates in their new stadium; yet at the same time they were paying big wages to players.

The trouble for Sittingbourne was that, in building their new stadium, they spent far more than the money they had received from the sale of the Bull ground and soon ran up large debts. Unable to maintain payment of the extravagant player salaries, results suffered on the pitch and Sittingbourne were forced to sell Central Park to Swale Council for a mere £750,000. By 1998 the club had gone into liquidation and Swale Council had locked the club out of the ground for non-payment of rent. Sittingbourne's salvation arrived in the form of an agreement between the council, the liquidators and, once more, financial support from the supporters. Sittingbourne saw out the 1990s surviving on a match by match basis.

The financial situation remained bleak for Sittingbourne into the new millennium and the team struggled on the pitch. Season 2000-01 saw an all time low as they were almost relegated to the Kent League. Before the start of the 2002-03 campaign the club decided to move out of the high-maintenance Central Park and took up residence on the adjacent training pitch. A summer of dedicated work by an army of volunteers resulted

Game 2 Sittingbourne 1 Chertsey Town 0

in the development of the new Bourne Park ground, where they play today. The huge Central Park Greyhound Stadium, with its impressive gates, large car park, and acres of surrounding space, still remains.

On my visit to Bourne Park, the club itself could not have been any more welcoming. Friendly faces, jovial turnstile operators, amicable programme sellers. Before the game I even got a mention on the tannoy, and this blog address was read out to the 190+ crowd. Quite a nice moment for me, but nothing too momentous for the crowd (there was no frenzied applause, for example). An old chap stood just alongside me had patently misheard the announcement and, with great concern, asked why there was a delay.

The game itself was by no means a classic. Sittingbourne just about deserved the victory in a match with few clear chances. Chertsey had a golden opportunity in the first half, when the right full-back (Billy Jones) was unable to connect with a cross as the goal stood empty in front of him. Sittingbourne looked the far more likely to score and this they did on 58 minutes when Lee Browning finished off a well worked move. Yours truly had the 72 minute Golden Goal ticket.

I managed to watch the game from a variety of different positions, with the most intriguing vantage point just in front of the tractor in one corner of the ground. Considering the amount of space outside and around the ground, it was a strange place to keep a tractor. But hey, what do I know about tractors? Maybe they like football too.

The game drifted to its conclusion with little further incident of any consequence, and the locals seemed more than happy with the result. It had been a lovely sunny day with a cooling breeze, and watching an FA Cup tie in these conditions didn't really compute. The skies were still big and blue with gigantic rolling clouds and a Wembley Final felt a million years away.

All in all a good afternoon out. A great little club who are striving to

Game 2 Sittingbourne 1 Chertsey Town 0

leave their financial problems firmly in the past, and if Sittingbourne now go on a bit of a Cup run there is a chance that I could be back here in a later round. I for one would be more than happy to return.

Sittingbourne v Liverpool would be good.

Pie in the sky?

Draw for the First Qualifying Round: Dartford v Sittingbourne

As I made my way back to the car, I could just about make out another tannoy announcement, this time about Sittingbourne's away game opponents in the next round. There was a huge cheer from the departing crowd and it was at that moment I realised I would be on my way back to this county for a Kent derby in two weeks time.

All Four Corners

In six days I'll be off to Dartford for the First Qualifying Round game against Sittingbourne. Whilst I'm looking forward to the game, there is something else that is quite engrossing about this venture. Yes, there will be many new grounds to visit. Yes, there will be teams I would not ordinarily travel to watch. Yes, there will be some cracking Cup football. But there is another thing, and I can't quite put my finger on it.

The only way I can describe the feeling is something akin to an adventure into the unknown. Admittedly, it is not in the same league as Tenzing and Hillary or Amundsen, but for me it is enthralling nonetheless. Just where in the country is this road to take me? The FA Cup draws will now have a completely different meaning for me. No longer will I simply be focused on my team. There will now be a totally new meaning. The balls pulled out of the bag could push me off almost anywhere in England or Wales. It is this I find the most captivating.

Sad, I know.

Out of interest, I took a look at the FA Cup competition from last season, 2006-07. Starting with Chertsey Town, I plotted the route to Wembley. The following sequence of games were thrown up:

Chertsey Town 3, Abingdon Town 2
Oxford City 5, Chertsey Town 0
Bishop's Cleeve 3, Oxford City 1
Newport County 4, Bishop's Cleeve 2
Tonbridge Angels 0, Newport County 1
Newport County 1, Swansea City 3
Darlington 1, Swansea City 3
Sheffield United 0, Swansea City 3
Ipswich Town 1, Swansea City 0

All Four Corners

Watford 1, Ipswich Town 0
Plymouth Argyle 0, Watford 1
Watford 1, Manchester United 4 (at Aston Villa)
Chelsea 1, Manchester United 0

And now it strikes me. If I had done this last season, I could have been off to all four corners... Newport, Darlington, Ipswich and Plymouth. I would have witnessed Swansea City's impressive Cup run. Interestingly, I would not have seen an all-Premiership tie until the Semi-Final, assuming I would have been able to find tickets.

But the past is no guide to the present, especially with the FA Cup.

Who knows? This season, I may spend the majority of the FA Cup in Kent.

Green Football

I've never really associated football with humanity's drive to save the planet. And I'm sure I would be excused for never even connecting the two. In fact, if there's ever a fraternity that is working hardest to increase the size of the gaping hole in the ozone layer, I'd guess it would be the football set. The power consumption on match days, the floodlight wattage, the noise pollution (except at the Arsenal library), the size of the water bill (both watering the pitch and filling the post match bath). And then the players with their fuel guzzling sports cars and the WAGs with their 4x4s. Not to mention all those air miles. Oblivion here we come.

But down at Dartford FC, carbon footprints are a serious matter.

Ten years ago if someone had told me they'd gone green, I'd tell them to lie down, don't make any sudden movements and I'd call a doctor. Nowadays, you're considered a miscreant if you don't recycle. All of sudden, out of nowhere, green is the nation's favourite colour.

In our house we recycle like there's no tomorrow. We have a box for newspapers, a bag for clothes. We take trips to the bottle bank to deposit plastic, we take trips to post glass. Cans in one bag, shoes in another. We compost. Endless sojourns to the foot of the garden, armed with vegetable peelings, fruit trimmings, tea bags and egg shells. Grass, leaves, shredded paper. Toilet roll tubes. And we save electricity. We've installed energy saving light bulbs and have turned the thermostat down by a couple of degrees.

It's great in our house, as long as you don't mind the dark and the cold. Our little bit to protect the polar ice caps.

Down at Princes Park, Dartford are doing their own little bit. Except

Green Football

their little bit is a pretty big bit. And impressive too. The football ground is the UK's first sustainable stadium; it is built from renewable timber and has a grass roof. The stadium is sunk two metres below ground level to reduce noise and light pollution. An average football pitch needs 20,000 litres of water a day but Dartford have two lakes to feed the pitch; solar panels generate sufficient energy to power the facilities. Funded by Dartford Borough Council, it is acclaimed to be one of the finest non League stadiums around.

On the eve of my trip to Kent it is this aspect I find most intriguing. Has it really got a grass roof? Wow, certainly a first for me!

Oh, and I'm going down with two good friends (PB and Posh Mate) tomorrow and we'll be travelling in the same car. Our own extra little bit to minimise ozone depletion. But what they don't know is that I need to drop some plastic bottle tops off at the Recycling Centre on the way...

Dartford 1 Sittingbourne 1
First Qualifying Round Saturday 15 September 2007
Attendance 870
Distance travelled 97 miles

Planning the journey for this game, it seemed ever so straightforward. Forty odd miles around the M25, off at junction 1b, left and left again. Piece of cake. But somehow we ended up stuck on Dartford's one-way system with all the Saturday afternoon bargain hunters. You've heard of the ship of fools? This was the car of idiots.

However, this was only a minor blip and some expert navigational skills soon had us at Princes Park with time to spare. We were marshalled into the car park by a Liam Gallagher look-a-like and pulled up outside what can only be described as a very impressive ground. It was a hot, sunny afternoon and the newness of the ground dazzled in the bright light. The place looked very fresh and clean; it still felt new and even smelt new.

Once inside the ground (after a quick look around the club shop) I was struck by the design. It has a modern, ergonomic feel, lots of contoured wood and glass. It is pleasing on the eye. At the risk of being unkind to Sittingbourne, the contrast in grounds could not have been more stark. More Ikea than Woolworths.

The club bar is pretty smart as well, with large plasma TV screens, a pool table and gallery overlooking the pitch. And what a great idea to display famous quotes from players on the bar walls, including one of my all-time favourites from Ian Rush: "I couldn't settle in Italy, it was like living in a foreign country".

So to the match. The game started at a frenetic pace, and the first half was very good. Dartford had a number of chances and seemed to unnerve the Sittingbourne defence from the off, and indeed took an early lead on 13 minutes with a well-executed lob by Jay May. Soon after they hit the post, and with the away team's defence looking decidedly unsettled I expected a hat full of goals. To Sittingbourne's credit, they themselves looked very dangerous on the break; they had pace on the wings and

23

Game 3   Dartford 1   Sittingbourne 1

managed on a number of occasions to get behind the Dartford back line. However, with only a lone striker up front, they failed to reap any reward. At the half-time whistle, Dartford just about deserved to be in front.

A trip to one of the refreshment bars during the interval was rather surreal. Having ordered a Cheese & Onion pasty, we watched three young girls behind the counter prod and poke a number of pastry wrapped offerings in an attempt (I guess) to find the Cheese & Onion variety. They looked rather confused (bless) but a prolonged attack on one pasty with a small stick seemed to convince the server that the said Cheese & Onion had been found. My friends in the meantime ordered meat pies which turned out to be Cornish Pasties. My Cheese & Onion specimen contained large chunks of chicken and mushroom. Keep trying girls...

The second half seemed to be played at a completely different pace. I guess the hot weather took its toll (the referee called for two water breaks) and all the hustle and bustle slowly ebbed from the game. Dartford failed to make their superiority count, and as the afternoon drew to a close you could sense that Sittingbourne may well get back into the game. This they did when Mitchell Sherwood struck a low shot to the keeper's right on 85 minutes. That's how it ended, 1-1. And yes, you've guessed it, another trip around the M25 to Kent for me for Tuesday's replay.

Overall a very enjoyable first visit to Dartford. The crowd of 870 must have been slightly disappointing, the smallest attendance ever at Princes Park to watch Dartford. But still a good turnout for a club playing at this level. There are a number of Blue Square Premier clubs who would be happy with a crowd that size. The ground would not look out of place at Blue Square Premier level, or perhaps even higher. It is evident after visiting Princes Park that Dartford have big aspirations.

But in the short term, they need to get past Sittingbourne in the FA Cup. And sort out their pasties.

Game 3   Dartford 1   Sittingbourne 1

Draw for the <u>Second Qualifying Round</u>: Dartford or Sittingbourne v Camberley Town.

Don't get me wrong, I've nothing against Kent, but come on, somebody is having a laugh! Having already seen games at Sittingbourne (Preliminary Round) and Dartford (First Qualifying Round), I will be off to Sittingbourne again for the replay on Tuesday.

The draw for the Second Qualifying Round was made today and, low and behold, it will be Dartford or Sittingbourne v Camberley Town. Another trip to Kent. My fourth trip to Kent. I have an awful feeling I have done all this before.

Sittingbourne 1 Dartford 5

First Qualifying Round replay Tuesday 18 Sept. 2007
Attendance 303
Distance travelled 131 miles

There is something extra special about a midweek football game under floodlights. Some of my earliest memories as a child are of watching Cup games on TV, midweek games played out in front of packed (standing) crowds. The teams would be illuminated from all four corners of the ground, with the players being followed around the pitch by their surreal four bodied shadows. And some classic games always spring to mind. Without giving my age away too much, I remember my Dad letting me stay up to watch the great European nights. I will never forget the Liverpool versus St. Etienne European Cup Quarter-Final. The red of Liverpool, the green of St. Etienne, the ginger of David Fairclough. Super-sub Fairclough coming on and scoring that late, late spectacular winning goal. The roar from the floodlit Kop that night could be heard three miles away. It makes the hairs stand up on the back of my neck.

And I'm not even a Liverpool fan.

Sittingbourne had their lights on for last night's replay against Dartford and as soon as I arrived, spying the illuminated ground in the distance, my childhood memories came flooding back. I've been to hundreds of evening games, and it's always the same. From Leeds to Luton, Preston to Peterborough. Always that sense of excitement at watching a game under floodlights. Superb.

There seemed to be a buzz around the ground as well, over 100 additional paying customers compared to my last visit to Bourne Park. There was a sizable contingent from Dartford, not surprising for the Kent neighbours.

Have I mentioned that this was my third trip to Kent...? I think I'm getting a bit paranoid about this.

My friend PB joined me for this trip, and he was befriended in the Gents

Game 4 Sittingbourne 1 Dartford 5

before the game by one of the stewards, who seemed keen to provide details of how to make a quick exit from the vicinity after the final whistle. Maybe the steward sensed it was going to be a tough game for the home team. I don't recall ever watching such a one-sided encounter. By half-time, Dartford were 4-0 up and the game was over. As the fourth goal hit the back of the net, the Sittingbourne keeper fell to ground and stayed down. He quickly realised that it was game over (for both him and his team); it later transpired he had broken a small bone in his knee.

Sittingbourne did not get a shot on target until the dying minutes of the game, when they were awarded a dubious penalty. Dartford totally dominated, and were stronger than their hosts in every department. A wonderful hat-trick from Brendon Cass (27, 44, 68 mins), plus goals from Adam Flanagan (23 mins) and Eddie McClements (36 mins) proved Dartford's superiority. It could quite easily have been more. The consolation goal from Bradley Spice arrived on 85 minutes.

As we were leaving after the game, I felt a little downhearted. I have seen Sittingbourne play three times in this Cup run, and visited Bourne Park twice, all within the space of a few weeks. I have to say that I have thoroughly enjoyed their company. I got another mention on the tannoy last night, and the match programme offered up a full page spread on my blog. The encouragement and support I received from Sittingbourne will stay with me for some time.

It is now time for Dartford to pick up the baton on this road to Wembley and it's an exit for Sittingbourne. Could the last one out please switch off the floodlights?

Revised draw for the Second Qualifying Round: Dartford v Camberley Town.

So, Camberley Town; another new team to talk about. Camberley play in the Combined Counties Premier League Division, a Level 9 club in the pyramid. Both Dartford and Sittingbourne are Level 8 clubs, and Chertsey Town (where I began my journey) are in the same League as

Game 4 Sittingbourne 1 Dartford 5

Camberley. As I write this Camberley sit third in their League with only one defeat after seven games. Along with Chertsey, Camberley entered this season's FA Cup at the Extra Preliminary Round and have so far disposed of Worthing United, Ash United and Colliers Wood United.

Romance Of The Cup

When I started out on this journey, I thought it was just going to be simply that; a physical journey through the FA Cup, from village to town to city culminating at Wembley. But I am slowly realising that I am also on another journey at the same time. A journey of discovery, understanding what the FA Cup really means to the clubs and to the players. The understanding that the FA Cup is actually all about the small clubs, the non League teams, who have one big chance to cause an upset, to go on their own little adventure into the later rounds. This is where the passion is. This is where the romance is. The hopes and the dreams.

True, these things exist when the League clubs enter the fray, but it is in these early stages of the FA Cup, in the Preliminary Rounds and in the Qualifying Rounds, where the sense that something special could happen is at its most heightened.

Glancing through the team names of clubs that entered this season's competition (731 in total) I see that there are some fantastic names. Blackpool Mechanics. Cammell Laird. Darlington Railway Athletic. Loughborough Dynamo. Norton & Stockton Ancients. Say these names out loud and they seem to evoke the amateur spirit of the competition. They are clubs that could not be any further removed from last season's Finalists, Chelsea and Manchester United.

And it is one of these team names that has caught my eye from the very early rounds; Wootten Bassett Town.

The name itself (to me anyway) conjures up images of the English countryside; the village green and pond, the church with its Sunday morning bells and cross of St. George. The pub next door. The half-timbered market hall. A thriving local community where the club is run and managed by the locals, most providing their services on a voluntary basis. Where the goalkeeper is also the local plumber. Where many of the players at the football club also turn out for the cricket team in the summer.

Grass roots football. This is where the FA Cup really means something. This is where the average man in the street, like you or I, can get the chance to play in the world's greatest Cup competition.

This has been the most illuminating part of my journey.

I now want to know where Wootten Bassett Town play. I find myself looking at their website on the internet. I am hooked. Although I have only been to three non League grounds so far on this road to Wembley, I have been sucked into the world of non League football through forums, message boards and contacts with a variety of clubs. Only yesterday I was asked to contribute to a publication called the 'Non-League Digest'. There is a huge following out there of teams who play at this level in front of crowds no bigger than 50. Wonderful.

The sad thing for me is that I know all this will come to an end. There will come a point in the season when my FA Cup baton passes from a non League team to a League team. Maybe in the First Round Proper. Maybe later. But it will end. At some stage, I will leave the non League world behind.

And the Cup adventures do eventually come to an end for all non League teams as well. This happened to Wootten Bassett Town, and in spectacular style. They had a great Cup run this year. They knocked out Highworth Town (big local rivals) and Bracknell Town (a huge scalp and a big Cup shock) before succumbing to Brockenhurst. They lost 5-1 at home. That disappointment was swiftly followed by a 12-0 defeat to Bournemouth in the FA Vase. Yes, you read it correctly; 12-0! Back down to earth with a huge thud.

Romance Of The Cup

So for Wootten Bassett Town the dream is over for this season. For me, I need to make the most of these Qualifying Rounds before the romance of the Cup quickly becomes a fading, distant memory.

Sensible Money

Well, tomorrow's game has come around rather quickly for me, and I'm looking forward to it. Dartford start the game as favourites, and it looks as if the sensible money will be on the home team. But you never know in the FA Cup.

Camberley Town are planning to take the usual coach for players and staff, plus an extra coach for supporters, so this should boost an already large home crowd. Dartford are more than capable of getting a crowd of over 1,000, as opposed to Camberley's average home gate of about 100. I'm still rather surprised that Dartford's attendance in the last round of this competition was the lowest ever at Princes Park, when you also consider it was against a Kent neighbour.

There is a debate going on at Dartford about the reason for the lower crowds in recent games. The consensus is that the youngsters are staying away (even though it is only £1 to get in for children). Dartford estimate that about 100 children no longer attend home games. Add on to that at least one accompanying parent and that is 200 no-shows. Pretty significant at this level.

How a club at this level markets itself, and attempts to attract local support, is critical to the success of the club. Camberley Town, only this week, have put out the call for ideas on how to attract paying customers, and again there seems to be an emphasis on youth.

But it is difficult these days when the kids have so many other choices. At the Dartford v Sittingbourne game, I lost count of the variety of different shirts that the youngsters were wearing. Chelsea, Charlton, West Ham, Arsenal and (most bizarrely) a Spurs shirt (poor child!). The glitz and glamour is only around the corner for many, and the non League clubs have this to compete against.

Sensible Money

My son loves playing football, but he's not over keen on watching the game. He resists any of my attempts to take him to Chertsey Town. He has attended a few Fulham games. He has a variety of different kits (e.g. England, Barcelona, RC Lens, PSV Eindhoven) but no single favourite. He claims to support one of Chelsea, Fulham, Manchester United or Liverpool - depending which friend he saw last. He is only seven years old, and kids are fickle at the best of times. I do not put any pressure on him to support any one particular team. He will make his own mind up in time, and chances are it will be based on who his friends and peers support.

And I would very much doubt that any of the sensible money would be on him choosing Chertsey, Sittingbourne, Dartford or Camberley.

Dartford 2 Camberley Town 2
Second Qualifying Round Saturday 29 September 2007
Attendance 906
Distance travelled 97 miles

A twisted ankle and a twist of fate.

Only a matter of hours after writing Friday's post on the eve of this game, I found myself taking my wife to the A&E department of St. Peter's Hospital, Chertsey. On the Friday lunchtime she had turned her ankle playing volleyball. It was a nasty accident, and as we helped her off the field my first reaction was that she had broken it. After a lengthy wait at the hospital, the X-ray showed that there was no break, but badly sprained ligaments. My wife now had a foot the size of a balloon and it was a nice shade of black to boot. We left A&E with my wife on crutches, in a lot of pain, and with instructions to rest with her feet up for a week. I was now at her beck and call and sensed it was going to be a very long week. At least she did not have a bell by her side with which to summon me...

Now, even before September is out, I had my first tough decision on this road to Wembley. Did I stay home and look after my wife or head off down the M25. Do I stay or do I go?

Well, I did what every good, caring, compassionate husband would have done... I went to the match.

We decided it would be best to take my son to the game, so giving my wife a bit of peace and quiet in the afternoon. And do you know what? My son was actually keen to go. Positively looking forward to it! Contrary to every single word I had written in my blog on the Friday. Shows what I know.

So, back on the M25 (it felt as if I'd never been away), my son chatting excitedly about the game and me feeling a little guilty.

The game itself was very good. It wasn't so much a Cup shock, but

34

Game 5 Dartford 2 Camberley Town 2

certainly a little tremor of a surprise. An excellent away draw for Camberley, who produced the two best goals I have seen so far in this FA Cup journey.

Dartford took an early lead (16 minutes) with a neat goal from Brendon Cass. From there on in Dartford seemed to do exactly as they did in the home game against Sittingbourne, which is squander any real chances they had. Intent on hitting long balls most of the time, completely by-passing midfield, they lost possession on too many occasions. Camberley seemed physically tiny compared to Dartford. I could have sworn one Camberley player was only about five foot tall. My son asked if he was their full back, Jason Short.

What Camberley lacked in height and physical presence they made up for with pace. Camberley certainly played better than I expected, and weren't afraid to have a go at Dartford. They began to find space for themselves and were rewarded on 27 minutes, when a beautifully struck 25 yard snap shot from Ben Cobbett brought the game level. 1-1 at half-time.

In the second half, Dartford began to bring their midfield into the game a little more and started to gain the upper hand; they won a series of corners and free kicks around the box at the height of their control. It was from one of these free kicks on the right that Dartford regained the lead. A high ball swung over caused a bit of panic in the Camberley box and it was nodded home by John Guest to make it 2-1 to Dartford. This after 55 minutes.

Dartford now were turning the screw, and Camberley's involvement in the game seemed to diminish. But, once more, Dartford failed to take their chances. A case of déjà vu.

And then, almost out of nothing, and with 15 minutes left on the clock, we were treated to a cracking goal from Camberley. A sweet strike from 30 yards, hit fully on the run by Dan Ker, gave the Dartford keeper Tony

Game 5 Dartford 2 Camberley Town 2

Kessell no chance whatsoever. With the game seemingly heading for another draw, Camberley may well have snatched a win late on when a cross into the Dartford box was just missed by the on-rushing forward. Now that would have been a smash and grab.

The exuberant manner in which Camberley Town celebrated both their goals and the final whistle demonstrated how much this result meant to the club. There is no doubt that they will be the happier of the two teams as both names go into the hat for Monday's Third Qualifying Round draw.

A couple of things happened at the game that accentuated the difference between this level of football and the higher echelons of the game, and both made me smile. Firstly, before the game started, there was a tannoy announcement reminding spectators that Princes Park was a no-smoking stadium. However, the gates would be opened at half-time for people to step outside for a smoke. Could you envisage the same flexibility at Old Trafford? And secondly, during the game, there was a stiff challenge on the touchline which propelled two players and the ball towards the perimeter fencing resulting in a gentleman in the crowd getting his hat knocked off. A pretty amusing bit of slapstick in its own right, but what made me smile was the Dartford defender who (on his way back to defend the quick throw) stopped and diverted his run to collect the said hat and return it to the supporter. A friendly gesture from a friendly club.

And there you have it; another replay and off down to Krooner Park on Tuesday evening. My son really enjoyed this game; there were even chants of "Come on you Darts!" from him during the match. I thoroughly enjoyed it as well, another great advert for non League football. Albeit my enjoyment was tinged with a little guilt. But by all accounts, my wife had a relaxing afternoon with her feet up.

And on that note, I'd best sign off. My wife is calling me. Something to do with wanting me to go out and buy her a bell.

Game 5 Dartford 2 Camberley Town 2

Draw for the <u>Third Qualifying Round</u>: Aylesbury United or Bromley v Dartford or Camberley Town.

Not conclusive, but one thing I know is that it won't be a trip to Kent for the next round - although I have to say that Bromley is dangerously close!

The Aylesbury v Bromley game on Saturday ended 1-1. The replay is on Tuesday evening, the same night as the Camberley v Dartford game. By late Tuesday I will know where I'm off to next, but I would be happy with either.

Camberley Town 0 Dartford 0
aet Dartford win 4-1 on penalties
Second Qualifying Round replay Tuesday 2 Oct. 2007
Attendance 242
Distance travelled 35 miles

Camberley on a miserable, wet, damp, dank, dark evening. A replay which simply did not live up to the first billing but ended with a few minutes of excitement in a penalty shootout. Dartford squeeze through, but only just. And about 150 Darts fans go home happy.

Four of us made the short journey to Camberley, and PB even came out especially for this game on his birthday. His 40th to be precise! Having already celebrated (drowned his sorrows) at reaching this mid-life point at the weekend, the draw of the FA Cup could not be resisted. Turning forty does strange things to a man's mind. You start to reflect on life past and life future. Some people struggle to deal with it. They do crazy things in an attempt to rekindle lost youth. Mid-life crisis. And last night, as PB saw out his 40th birthday in the drizzle at Krooner Park, it suddenly hit me.

Good God, I'm having my own mid-life crisis! This whole FA Cup thing. This is my black Porsche. This is my trek across the Andes. This is my long-legged brunette from accounts. You know, the one with the big personality. That explains everything. I feel I can justify this crazy venture. I'll be fine once I get through it and out the other side all in one piece, my marriage still intact and my family still talking to me. I'll be just fine. Phew.

Might as well enjoy it while it lasts!

Enjoyment is not a word I feel at ease using in the context of last night's game. But then again, maybe. The game was poor. But I still enjoyed the evening in a sad kind of way. You know what I mean; I'd rather be at a bad game of football than dozing in front of Eastenders. And the evening had its snippets of entertainment, which I'll come to later.

Game 6 Camberley Town 0 Dartford 0

But as for the game; it was, believe me, not very good. The pitch was very wet and heavy from a couple of days of constant drizzle. The kind of drizzle that is the poor relation to rain, it just kind of hangs in the air. Stand in it long enough and your skin starts to wrinkle.

The Camberley ground was very much like Chertsey's ground, probably fairly typical at this level. One main stand, a single turnstile entrance, a small refreshments hut, an ageing bar. One end was partially covered with a wooden roof which provided shelter, a good view of the pitch and an equally good view of the club car park behind. The Camberley folk were friendly and welcoming. I take my hat off to two young girls who were selling raffle tickets before the game. They were brave enough to walk around the ground and into the travelling Dartford fans calling out "£1 a strip". Well, I assume it was raffle tickets they were selling.

No goals in normal time or extra-time and that kind of sums the game up. In the first half, only one significant event to comment on; the sending off of Dartford's Jay May for kicking out at a Camberley player after he was felled with a tackle from behind. The rest of the half was really a non-event. Lots of misplaced passes, long hoofs out of defence, rough tackles and hard challenges. And a great deal of niggle between the two sets of players, which seemed to have spilled over from the first game last Saturday. I guess this had a part to play in the sending off. To see this kind of hard, uncompromising football, up close and almost within touching distance, can make for quite a spectacle. Poor football, but entertaining nonetheless.

The second half saw Camberley attacking down the slope toward the end we stood at. All the Dartford fans (who had provided the best entertainment in the first half) had swapped ends and were just visible in the half light and drizzle a pitch length away. This made for a quiet half for us and I hate to admit it was quite painful to watch. The only positive to come from the game was that Camberley started to play some football on the deck, and for this they looked the more likely to score. The Dartford fans in the distance were getting more and more frustrated

Game 6 Camberley Town 0 Dartford 0

with the standard of refereeing and some of the delaying tactics of the Camberley players, but other than that there wasn't a great deal to shout about.

Camberley did have an opportunity to score with just under 70 minutes on the clock when a high ball into the box evaded the keeper and fell to an unmarked Camberley forward. It seemed easier for him to score into the unguarded net than miss, but he somehow pulled his shot across goal and beyond the far post. As the game stumbled towards extra-time, my friends started to pray for a goal. An additional 30 minutes would be difficult to take.

Nil-nil at 90 minutes (more like 97 minutes with all the injury time, where did that come from?) and into extra-time. The Dartford fans began to make their way back to our end as the players lined up to kick-off. At the last moment, the players swapped ends which meant that Dartford were now kicking away from us. Some Dartford fans realised this and carried out an about-turn manoeuvre, whilst others carried on regardless. This caused a rather amusing mass crowd collision around about the half-way line. I think this was probably the highlight of the match. I'm glad to report there were no serious injuries.

The extra thirty minutes went by quite quickly, with Dartford having the best chance in the last few minutes when John Guest missed from all of five yards. It was to be one of those nights. Still no goals. And so to penalties.

Jamie Coyle, Steve Norman, Eddie McClements and Adam Flanagan all scored from the spot for Dartford. Camberley scored their first penalty; Tony Kessell in the Dartford goal saved two. As Flanagan sealed the tie with the winning kick, the Dartford fans (now down at our end) went berserk and the Dartford players, subs, manager, coach, physio, coach driver and tea lady ran to the Dartford fans to join in the celebrations. An exciting end to a poor game.

Game 6 Camberley Town 0 Dartford 0

Over the two games, I think Dartford deserved to go through. Last night they defended resolutely with ten men when they needed to, a task made harder by the heavy pitch. I felt a little sorry for Camberley as they did try to play some decent football in the second half and they must surely be agonising over that missed chance late on.

Revised draw for the <u>Third Qualifying Round</u>: Bromley v Dartford.

Meanwhile, on the same evening, Bromley were disposing of Aylesbury United in their replay; final score 4-2 after extra-time. This now sets up a Bromley v Dartford Third Qualifying Round game on Saturday 13th October.

I can't wait. I need to crack on with my mid-life crisis.

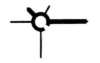

Is Bromley In Kent?

Don't answer that question. Not just yet.

For those of you who have been following my story, I have spent an awful lot of time in Kent so far. No problem with that, but it would be nice to see some new counties. After the draw for the Third Qualifying Round, I made a comment about Bromley not being in Kent. I didn't put much (if any) thought into this comment as I wrote it. Engage brain before you write.

But, my word, what a reaction I have had to that single comment. I have probably had more correspondence and read more columns of message board and forum space about that remark compared to anything else I've written to date.

And I'm all for it. The debate has been quite lively, most entertaining and in many cases very amusing. In essence it boils down to whether Bromley is in the county of Kent or resides in Greater London. The more complex arguments have touched on post codes, boundary changes, borough councils, administrative areas and the like. Oh, did I also mention all this has been most educational for me?

My initial reaction was to go and do a bit of research for myself. That's me in a nutshell; the methodical, predictable, 'black v white' type of person. I found that the more definitive sources suggest Bromley is not in Kent, although it used to be before boundary changes in 1965. It is now a London borough and Bromley resides in the 'Ceremonial County' of Greater London. I even contacted the Kent Tourist Board, who also stated that Bromley is no longer in Kent.

The counter arguments are based around postal addresses. For example, take a look at the Bromley FC website; their address (displayed at the

Is Bromley In Kent?

foot of the home page) quite clearly states "Bromley, Kent". It is like this for many other businesses and locations in and around Bromley. The excellent 'Kentish Football' website includes coverage of Bromley, so one assumes they also believe Bromley is in Kent.

So, not that conclusive, but I was starting to favour the Greater London answer. But then it was a comment I read this morning on the Pure DFC Forum (Dartford FC's Unofficial Discussion Site) that made me realise I was looking at this from completely the wrong angle:

"I guess it's officially the London Borough of Bromley, but anybody from the area will tell you it's Kent".

There was I trying to determine whether it was Kent or not, looking for an 'official' and 'authoritative' answer, when this quote made everything crystal clear. Suddenly I see. At the end of the day, it doesn't really matter. The official answer is not that important.

What is important is what people believe. What the citizens of Kent believe. What Bromley town's folk believe. And it's all to do with regional identity. This is what defines you, where you come from, where you grew up, where you now live or where you used to live. It is in your blood. It is what makes you, well, you. If Bromley used to be Kent, then why can't it still be Kent if that's what people perceive?

Trying tell residents of the Basque region they are Spanish. Try telling the Cherokee Nation that they are really Americans. Try telling inhabitants of the Faroe Islands that they live in Denmark. All rather extreme examples I know, but you get my point? From everything I have read I get the sense that Kent people are very proud of their county, proud to come from Kent. So should I really be judging whether Bromley is in Kent or not? Who am I to question regional identity?

And so to answer that question; yes, I will be off to Kent for the next game on Saturday 13th October. Bromley v Dartford. I know the way.

Don't Believe Everything You Read

Towards the end of last week I picked up a copy of our 'freebie' newspaper, the instantly forgettable 'Walton and Weybridge Informer'. You know, the weekly that is pushed through your front door whether you want it or not. Ninety percent of the newspaper is made up of adverts, and most of the stories are truncated so that if you are really interested you have to read the full story in the sister newspaper, the Surrey Herald (75p).

Now the reason I mention this is that, on the back page, there was a picture from a Chertsey Town match. In one of my very earliest posts you may recall that I was bemoaning how little (if any) coverage Chertsey Town get in the local press. You would be excused for believing that the town did not have a football team. The back page of the 'Informer' is usually devoted to Esher Rugby Club. To have a picture from a Chertsey Town match was, to say the least, unusual.

There was no accompanying report with it, only the picture. The picture caption read: "Scott Edgar (right) rolls in Chertsey's third goal in Saturday's 3-0 FA Cup win against Erith".

Now, as you know, Chertsey were eliminated from the FA Cup at Sittingbourne on 1st September in the Preliminary Round after beating Wick in the Extra Preliminary Round. So to see a picture from their FA Cup triumph (in October) against Erith Town was all rather... baffling?

An obvious error, but it got me thinking. I wonder how many people believe Chertsey are still in the FA Cup? There may well be a small group of Chertsey fans who are walking around town revelling in Chertsey's greatest ever FA Cup run. They may need expert help; the emotional trauma of the truth may be too much to bear. It saddens me just to think of it.

Don't Believe Everything You Read

This error now makes me question the accuracy of the local paper's BIG news stories. Did the 'Friend's of Chertsey Library' really raise £13.78 at their coffee morning, with cakes made by Ethel and Mavis? Did callous thieves really steal the life size papier-mâché model of Bruce Forsyth from the local craft shop? The same papier-mâché model that was found two days later balanced precariously atop the church flag pole. Was Chesney Hawkes really the guest of honour at the Black Cherry Fair? How do I know that any of this is true? It may well all have been utter fabrication or, at best, unmitigated errors.

Everything I once believed in I must now question. My whole value system is in tatters. I'm going to write a letter of complaint to the editor. No doubt they will only print part of it.

So it just goes to show, don't believe everything you read.

Except this blog. Obviously.

Divided We Stand

At the Bromley v Dartford game tomorrow you will find several hundred Bromley fans, several hundred (very noisy) Dartford fans and at least one Sunderland fan, a Peterborough United fan and a Leeds United fan. The odd ones out in that sentence are the teams of choice of the three of us travelling to Hayes Lane for this FA Cup Third Qualifying Round game. And the great thing about tomorrow's game is that all paying customers will be standing together. There will be no segregation. Supporters of both participants will mingle freely before, during and after the game. All genuine football fans with a shared passion for the game.

One of the definite highlights on this FA Cup road so far has been the lack of segregation at the grounds. Fans have still grouped together and swapped ends at half-time, which is only natural. Tribal instinct prevails. But I have stood amongst Sittingbourne and Chertsey fans as they traded good humoured jibes with each other. I have stood between Dartford and Sittingbourne supporters as both groups bemoaned the quality of refereeing. I have stood at one end of Camberley's ground and spent alternate halves of normal and extra-time standing with either the home support or the away support.

After my son came with me to watch the Dartford v Camberley game, I was surprised how much he enjoyed it. I asked him why, when at other games he had become bored or twitchy long before the players were tucking into their half-time oranges. The answer didn't really surprise me. He enjoyed the freedom of being able to move around the terrace and watch the game from a variety of different vantage points. He enjoyed not being confined to one seat for a full ninety minutes. He didn't feel trapped.

I saw a question raised about the Bromley game tomorrow; would there be segregation at this game? It is a fair question as a big crowd is

Divided We Stand

expected. Bromley have stated that there will not be any segregation.

Good news.

I wonder how long into this FA Cup journey I will travel before I encounter a game where fans are forced to stand apart. Possibly in the First Round Proper when the League clubs enter the fray. A friend of mine has already asked where I would stand for segregated games; the home or away end? To be honest, I don't know. In the latter rounds I'm sure it will be where ever I can get a ticket.

Thinking of all my family, friends and work colleagues who are into football, the range of football teams that they support is quite large. I've already mentioned Sunderland, Peterborough United and Leeds United. QPR and Fulham have also been represented on this FA Cup journey. Other teams supported in my social coterie include Manchester United and Manchester City, Liverpool, Crystal Palace, Arsenal, Nottingham Forest, Marlow, Altrincham, Aldershot, Hereford United, Hull City, Wolverhampton Wanderers, Coventry City, Newcastle United, Stockport County, Sheffield United, Newport County, Cwmbran Town... I could go on. The point is that we all have been to watch games with our friends and enjoy doing so, irrespective of who is playing.

And irrespective of where you stand or sit.

Tomorrow we will have a choice of where to stand. I just hope I'm not stood next to any weird Sunderland or Peterborough United fans.

Bromley 1 Dartford 0
Third Qualifying Round Saturday 13 October 2007
Attendance 1,022
Distance travelled 96 miles

Stepping into Bromley's ground felt like stepping back in time. The club was founded in 1892 and moved to Hayes Lane in 1938 and I'd hazard a guess that, with the exception of the new John Fiorini Stand and several coats of black tar and paint, little has changed. Much of the old ground is black and white. There are two black stands at either end of the ground each with white supports; black benches behind one goal; white barriers on the terracing with one of the terraces being completely open down the length of the ground. The club colours are black and white. Many Bromley supporters were adorned with the old fashioned long, knitted, black and white striped scarves. Relics from years gone by (the scarves that is, not the supporters).

All this seemed to create an evocative and nostalgic air to the place. The club shop window (within the ground) displayed ageing black and white and sepia toned photographs of past glories. Pictures of big, proud footballers peering through the mists of time in their big leather boots and big shorts. Even older team shots with players sporting between-the-war caps, the obligatory football middle centre with its big laces.

I liked the place as soon as I walked into it, and I don't recall visiting a football ground that felt so immersed in it's past. The PA announcer added to this ambience; the Mr Cholmondley-Warner voice evoking memories of post-war radio football and FA Cup Finals played out in black and white. I thought I even heard the sound of an odd rattle or two echo around the old stands. In many years time I'm sure I'll remember yesterday's match in monochrome, a variety of shades of grey.

What a glorious day it was to enjoy the game. Sunny and short-sleeve shirt warm, not bad for October. The supporters were out in force, over 1000 including an estimated 400+ from Dartford. And we were all treated to a good game of football.

Game 7 Bromley 1 Dartford 0

The 1-0 scoreline suggests that there was little between the teams, and this was almost the case, but not quite. Dartford did well against a Bromley team who looked very comfortable on the ball. Playing their League football at two levels above Dartford, Bromley seemed to have a lot more time on the ball and managed to regularly find that extra yard of space. I always felt that Bromley would win this tie, but they didn't seem to finish Dartford off as easily as their dominance suggested. And in all honesty, they were dominant without totally domineering. Strange thing to say I know, but they didn't quite take a strangle-hold on the game. Yes, Bromley had lots of possession. Yes, they made the better use of the big pitch. Yes, they stroked the ball around technically well and confidently. But at the end of it all they failed to turn their superiority into goals.

And this allowed Dartford to have some spells in the game whereby they may well have contrived to snatch a draw. Dartford resorted to hitting Bromley on the break, but Dartford's lack of firepower up front resulted in few shots that really tested the Bromley keeper. The only sign of weakness for Bromley was their rather static back three (or was it five?) and Dartford managed on a few occasions to get behind them. Unfortunately for Dartford they failed to inflict any damage.

On the 55th minute Bromley were awarded a penalty when a strong flat run across the edge of the area was unceremoniously ended with a hearty man and ball challenge just inside the box which left the referee with little choice but to point to the spot. The incident occurred at the opposite end from where we were standing so it was difficult to say if it was a valid penalty or not. There seemed to be little protest from the Dartford players. Danny Hockton took the kick which was well saved by Tony Kessell but Hockton pounced on the rebound to turn it into the net.

The goal seemed to spark a little more life into Dartford. The Dartford fans upped the noise level and the away team regained some control of the game. But as in the first half, they lacked any quality in the final third

Game 7   Bromley 1   Dartford 0

and just couldn't lay off the killer pass. Andy Walker in the Bromley goal had very little to do. At the same time, Bromley seemed to be cruising in a lower gear; they played some neat football out from the back and most of their game was calm and controlled. One always sensed that Bromley were perhaps a little too laid back, and a late equaliser from Dartford always seemed feasible. But this never came. Bromley finished with a flourish and a couple of very good saves from Kessell kept the score at 1-0. Overall just about a fair result, but only just. I was particularly impressed with Bromley's nippy little number 11, Sam Wood, who possessed a great deal of pace and never stopped running for the cause. Kessell in the Dartford goal also played his part. A good Cup game.

At the final whistle we headed for the bar to watch England stroll past Estonia; a great way to finish off the visit. The new stand and bar at Hayes Lane are quite impressive, but I'm not sure why they put the two Plasma TV screens in such awkward to watch positions behind the bar. Ho hum.

And so my FA Cup road to Wembley baton now passes to Bromley. And sadly, it is goodbye to Dartford.

I have seen Dartford play five times on this run and I feel as if I have grown to know the club a little. Their supporters are a great advert for the game in the lower Leagues. They support their team in numbers both home and away, are most vocal and have been a great bunch to correspond with.

At this point I must say hello to 'custdart' and 'eagle88' both of whom I met at the game yesterday. Thank you for your very kind comments about this blog, it means a lot to me. I'm sorry to see Dartford go out. One thing I do know is that there is every chance I will pay a visit to Princes Park again in the future. My son keeps nagging me!

And now onward with Bromley. With a ground that oozes a sense of the past, it is time for Bromley to look ahead and dream of a potential

Game 7 Bromley 1 Dartford 0

money-spinning FA Cup run. Only one more round before the First Round Proper. Bromley fans have every reason to be excited at what the future may bring.

And why not? After all, nostalgia is not what it used to be.

Draw for the <u>Fourth Qualifying Round</u>: Eastbourne Borough v Bromley.

One thing that I have not admitted to whilst writing this blog, is that deep down I have always hoped that this road would, at least once, lead me to the coast.

So following today's draw for the Fourth Qualifying Round of the FA Cup you could say that I am fairly chuffed with the outcome.

Your Football Club Wants You!

More than once in this blog I have mentioned the role volunteers play in local football. At clubs such as Chertsey Town, Sittingbourne and Camberley Town, where financial backing is scarce, the role of the volunteer cannot be understated. They are the life-blood of clubs and without them many would not survive. Across the length and breadth of the country this is evident; it drills right down into the heart of football in this country, even below the non Leagues. Into youth football, school football and Sunday park pub football.

I looked up the word volunteer in the dictionary. It is defined thus:

vol·un·teer – noun
1. a person who voluntarily offers himself or herself for a service or undertaking.
2. a person who performs a service willingly and without pay or reward.

Whenever I hear the word volunteer I think of the Battle of the Somme (July 1916) in the First World War. Not an obvious association you might think, but I have more than a passing interest in the battle which was one of the bloodiest in history. The reason I associate the word volunteer with this horror is that the majority of military personnel that died were volunteers of the Territorial Force and Horatio Kitchener's 'New Army'. Now the thing that fascinates me the most is the willingness of young men from all parts of the UK to give their lives in the name of their country. The willingness of young men with seemingly their whole lives ahead of them to step over the top into certain death. A sacrifice that, no matter how much I read about it or think about it, I still struggle to fathom.

Anyway, back to the football. Don't believe for a second that I am comparing the voluntary work that goes on in our national game with

Your Football Club Wants You!

the giving of life in the First World War (or any other war for that matter). The two are beyond approach. But the part of the definition that stands out for me is that volunteers 'give freely' and 'without personal reward'. And down at Eastbourne Borough, this is happening to an extent that has really taken me by surprise.

I guessed that the degree of help given freely within the local community would dissipate the further up the pyramid one progressed. Eastbourne Borough are, after all, joint top of the Blue Square South (as I write this), only two steps away from the Football League. I had every reason to believe that the set up at Eastbourne Borough would be a little more 'full-time' than that witnessed at clubs in the earlier rounds.

How wrong could I have been?

Eastbourne Borough FC only have one paid employee (the Commercial Manager) and she only works four days a week. There is no one bankrolling the club and the club relies on a team of dedicated volunteers. There is also a full-time Bar Steward employed by the Sports Club but that's it. Other bar staff are part time and nearly every other person at the club (including the Chairman, Chief Executive, all the Committee and the match-day Stewards) offer their services freely.

Eastbourne Borough is a 'members' club' which means that it is owned by the members. Membership of the club committee is open as long as interested parties have the skills (and time) required to help run the club. No one individual has any financial interest and any 'profits' that are made go straight back into the club. The club is also an important centre of the community. They provide adult education; a nursery for foundation learning; a bowls and an archery club; plus a massive youth section comprising of approximately 500 boys and girls in over 40 different teams.

Eastbourne Borough for the best part of their history have been a sports and community club. In 1964 Langney Football Club was founded,

Your Football Club Wants You!

taking their name from nearby Langney Point. Indeed, the Langney Point Martello Tower is an image represented on the club crest; one of a series of Martello Towers along the South Coast which date from the Napoleonic Wars.

Four years later the club became Langney Sports Club with affiliation to Langney Community Association. In 2001 the name of Eastbourne Borough was adopted. Many of the people who played in a youth team in the 1960s have since stayed together, formed the club, built the ground and built the clubhouse themselves. Much of the money raised has come from their own fund raising efforts and many still serve the needs of the club.

I have been invited to have a look behind the scenes at Eastbourne Borough and I am honoured and intrigued in equal measure. By all accounts the Chairman and Vice Chairman will (before the game this time next week) be laying bricks for the smokers' shelter outside the club bar.

And one last thing; I must question the 'without reward' element in my earlier definition of the word 'volunteer'.

In the case of Eastbourne Borough there is reward. The results of all the hard work and effort by the band of volunteers at Eastbourne Borough are tangible. The actual existence and continued survival of the club is due, in no small measure, to the time and dedication of the volunteers within the community. A real altruistic contribution in every sense of the word. There is a genuine sense of pride and community spirit that oozes out of Eastbourne Borough Football Club.

And I haven't even been there yet!

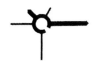

Go The Distance

Ahead of Saturday's journey to the South Coast, I have travelled a total distance of 587 miles. Which is less than a return trip between Torquay (Devon) and York (erm, Yorkshire...).

So what?

Well, on Sunday evening I watched, courtesy of Setanta (or is it Sultana?), the Blue Square Premier League contest between York City and Torquay United. My first reaction was simply this: why on earth is this fixture between two teams that are physically distanced by a total of 314.5 miles being played on a Sunday evening? That is a round trip of 629 miles for the Devon faithful. On a Sunday evening. Who in their right mind would schedule that?

Setanta, that's who.

It will come of little surprise that this caused some upset at Torquay. When the League fixtures were announced in the summer, this game was scheduled for a normal Saturday afternoon slot. Actually, scratch that. Nowadays Saturday afternoon slots are becoming less and less the norm. Anyway, good news for the travelling Torquay contingent. A 3pm kick-off on a Saturday. No problem.

Enter stage left Setanta. Game moved to a Tuesday evening. Displeasure amongst the Torquay fans; plans rearranged, weekend trips cancelled. New plans made. Exit stage right Setanta.

But hold on; enter back onto stage Setanta. A comedy entrance. The kind of 'funny-if-it-wasn't-so-true' comedy entrance. They've changed their minds. The game will no longer be on that Tuesday, but now on a Sunday at 7pm. Yes, that's it, 7pm. Perfect. No one will mind. Rearranged plans rearranged again. Cancelled weekend trips now become cancelled Tuesday evening trips. More disgruntled Torquay fans. Many cannot now travel to historic York. A Torquay fan from Sheffield cannot even make it across the county because the last train from York to Sheffield on a Sunday evening leaves just before the game ends.

During the game Setanta even have the audacity to step in amongst the Torquay fans to interview them during the game. Needless to say one of the questions was not "What time do you think you will get back home tomorrow morning?"

TV schedules are controlling the game to such an extent that kick-off times are barely recognisable anymore. Friday evening, Saturday morning, Saturday teatime, Sunday lunchtime, Sunday afternoon, Monday evening, Thursday evening. But a Sunday evening? That is a new one on me. Fans will (and do) find it harder to travel to games at obscure times, particularly where long distances are involved. And when the nation's public transport system just isn't up to scratch it can be virtually impossible.

My trip to Eastbourne Borough on Saturday will be my furthest single trip so far, but will still take under ninety minutes, traffic permitting. I know that from the First Round Proper onwards I could have some big distances to travel as the regionalisation disappears. I am prepared to go the distance.

I just hope my First Round Proper game will not be covered by Setanta.

Eastbourne Borough 2 Bromley 1
Fourth Qualifying Round Saturday 27 October 2007
Attendance 1,212
Distance travelled 160 miles

My first ever visit to Priory Lane, home of Eastbourne Borough. One thing I had been told about (or should I say 'warned' about) were the drums. The Eastbourne Borough drums, the favoured instruments of a small group of youngsters down one side of the ground. A never ending beat. All the way through the game. And they were damn noisy. But I must say they did actually contribute toward a good atmosphere, just as long as you stood at the opposite side of the ground to them. With the help of those drums, Eastbourne Borough beat a path into the First Round Proper of this prestigious competition.

Ever since their name was pulled out of the hat to face Bromley I have had a great response from Eastbourne Borough FC. I have already written a post on how the club is run by an immensely dedicated team of volunteers and of the sense of pride that emanates from the club. I was now looking forward to experiencing this first hand.

PB and I were asked to arrive at the club early so that we could be treated to a look behind the scenes. In all honesty, I expected nothing more than a quick fifteen minutes walk around the ground. Mainly because I appreciate how busy anyone involved with football clubs can be on match days. However, our host Lee Peskett (webmaster and committee member) gave us well over an hour from his busy schedule in what was a most fascinating and educational tour around Priory Lane.

Lee was an enthusiastic host. We were shown around the Langney Sports Club which sits adjacent to the ground and is an important part of the set up there. This included the Adult Training Suite and the Conference Room above, resplendent with framed national shirts from the 2006 Non League Four Nations Tournament (Priory Lane hosted all three England games). Into the Executive Boxes (in the Mick Green stand) which double up as home for the Owlets Nursery School during the weekdays. Into the Boardroom built onto the back of the main 542 seater stand which

Game 8   Eastbourne Borough 2   Bromley 1

also includes a couple of newer Boxes. We were kindly introduced to the Chairman and Commercial Manager and we witnessed first hand the amount of work that goes on behind the scenes long, long before the turnstiles clunk into action.

As if to exemplify the varied jobs those involved in the club have, when we met the Chairman he was hard at work on the construction of a smoking shelter outside the bar. I believe not long after he had to make a quick change into his suit to welcome the Bromley visitors.

We were also introduced to David Bauckham who took time out to meet us. Anyone involved in non League football, particularly in Sussex, will know David. He has also been involved with Eastbourne Borough for longer than he cared to share with us. We were later to see David writing up the team names on a white board displayed just beyond the turnstile entrance (a feature which was endearing in its own right) and off around the pitch to take match photographs.

Many involved with the club have indeed been involved for some time. I mentioned in an earlier post how the club was founded by members of the 1960s youth team. Some of these guys are still involved with the club today. The manager (Garry Wilson) came to the club in 1999 and the coach (Nick Greenwood) in 1997. Both have helped steer the club from Sussex County League football to the pinnacle of Blue Square South in a little over seven years. One of Eastbourne's players, Darren Baker, has made over 740 appearances.

It is this that impressed me most about the club; the length of time people have been around at Eastbourne. No fly-by-nights here looking for a quick buck or a moment in the spotlight. Instead, people who are truly committed to the club and the community and have been so for a very long time. I came away with an even greater understanding of how this club has developed as a community asset, how it has grown since the mid-sixties on the back of extremely well managed local effort, commitment and hard work. The club is justifiably proud of this.

Game 8 Eastbourne Borough 2 Bromley 1

Oh yes, I almost forgot. In amongst all this there was a game to report on. And not a bad game either. An impressive crowd of 1,212 included about 200 travelling Bromley fans. By way of comparison, Gretna only attracted a crowd of 1,020 for their game with Inverness Caledonian Thistle in the Scottish Premier League on the same day.

The first half was quite an even, if somewhat tense, affair; both sets of players were certainly up for it with strong, uncompromising physical challenges the order of the day. At times the referee struggled to keep control of this feisty encounter. Eastbourne Borough looked the more dangerous up front, and they took the lead after 27 minutes when Andy Atkin nodded in a cross. Eastbourne Borough missed a good chance to go 2-0 up before the break when Andy Walker saved easily from a weak, fluffed shot from only a few yards out.

In the second half, Eastbourne had the edge for the first ten minutes or so but failed to capitalise. The home team were given a wake-up call when their goalkeeper Lee Hook had to make a wonderful double save to deny efforts from Nic McDonnell and Barry Moore. But Bromley did not have to wait long. A route one ball played up field fell kindly to the on-rushing Garath McCleary who finished well to bring the scores level. 1-1 after 56 minutes.

Then on the hour Bromley's Mark Corneille received two quick bookings in the space of a few minutes for badly timed tackles. End of the game for Corneille, ironically a former Borough player. Strangely though, the reduction to ten men seem to galvanise the away team who dug deep, defended well and began to hit Eastbourne Borough on the break. Tactically, Eastbourne got it all wrong during this stage of the game. They had opportunity to make the most of the additional free space, but resorted to long balls. Possession was squandered all too easily and passes often misplaced.

Into the last quarter of the match and the draw looked increasingly likely with each passing minute. My thoughts soon turned to a Tuesday night

Game 8   Eastbourne Borough 2   Bromley 1

replay at Hayes Lane. But then a double substitution on 72 minutes by the home team seemed to change the complexion of the game. Eastbourne's passes were a little more accurate and attacks a little more assured. Bromley began to struggle with the lone striker and were forced to defend deeper and deeper.

But then a breakthrough. On 87 minutes Eastbourne were awarded a disputed penalty. My view is that I thought it was a dubious decision; two opposing players collided just inside the box with both players running away from goal. The referee all too quickly pointed to the spot. The resultant penalty kick was unceremoniously thumped into the onion bag by Paul Armstrong to send the home fans into raptures and the drummers into overdrive.

Two-one and Eastbourne Borough go through to the next round.

What a marvellous day. There is much more that I learnt about the minutiae of running a club such as Eastbourne Borough but I will save some of my thoughts about that for a future post.

We headed for the car after the game looking forward to the draw for the next round. And I must admit it was quite tense waiting to see who Eastbourne Borough would play and by association where fate would be sending me next. And I'm very pleased to report I will be back at Priory Lane in two weeks time to watch Eastbourne Borough take on either Weymouth or Hitchin Town. Another trip to the South Coast.

I drove home with a splitting headache with the pounding of those drums still resonating around my thick skull. I managed to call in at the local doctors on my arrival back in Chertsey for a quick diagnosis. Apparently, it was the worst case of percussion he had ever seen.

Draw for the First Round Proper: Eastbourne Borough v Weymouth.

As is to be expected, the further I progress through the rounds of this FA

Game 8 Eastbourne Borough 2 Bromley 1

Cup competition, the further up the pyramid one climbs. And after last night's replay win (1-0) for Weymouth away at Hitchin Town, a Blue Square Premier League club now enters the fray for the first time. My baton is with Eastbourne Borough, and they will host Weymouth in the FA Cup First Round Proper on Saturday 10th November.

Don't Take Anything For Granted

There are many things in life we know will happen: night follows day; we are born; and we will die. We pay tax. Our knees will eventually give up on us. These are certainties.

Then again there are things in life I take for granted, which I know I should not. Water. Electricity. My wife. My family. My health. Sugar.

There are things in life that perhaps we should do, but never do: enjoy your youth before it's too late; do one thing every day that scares you; and don't worry about the future. Dance. Sing. Floss.

In football there are perceived certainties. We know that one of Manchester United, Liverpool, Chelsea or Arsenal will win the Premier League this season. Maybe not? We are certain that England will lose the next penalty shoot out they are involved in. Who knows? We can say confidently that a club outside of the Premier League will not win the FA Cup in the next ten years. Who can say? Maybe in this beautiful game there are no real certainties. In reality these are things we are just taking for granted.

Regular readers will no doubt have gathered that the FA Cup is my favourite football competition. There are certain things I have always taken for granted. The excitement of the games; the David v Goliath match-ups; the Cup shocks; the fact that the BBC always chose to televise a dull all-Premier League tie in the Third Round. And the thrill at the small clubs when a big team comes a visiting.

On the eve of the Eastbourne Borough v Bromley match last week, the FA allocated draw numbers for clubs that would be in the hat for the First Round Proper. And there will be some big names in the draw, Leeds United and Nottingham Forest the most notable.

Don't Take Anything For Granted

I have always assumed that if you spoke to anyone involved with a non League club they would positively drool at the thought of a big club coming to town. But during my visit to Eastbourne Borough, a comment from committee member Lee Peskett really caught me on the blind side. It made me question something I had always taken for granted.

I put this question to Lee: "I guess you fancy Leeds or Forest at home in the next round then?" I felt at the time that this was a rhetorical question. Goes without saying doesn't it?

But no, it doesn't. Lee painted the picture for me. Yes, a home tie against a big club would be great. The fans would love it. It would be a proud moment for the club. It would capture the imagination of the town. And so on; things we hear every season at this stage of the competition. But there was a but. A big but.

For a small club, drawing a big team at home could be a logistical nightmare.

Lee pointed out that there are many additional things that need to be considered if a big team comes to town. One is segregation. This does not simply involve throwing up a gate between two sections of ground. It has to be installed to meet all of the Health and Safety standards. The segregated fans must have safe access in and out of the ground. Refreshment and toilet facilities need to be made available. Things we take for granted at the top grounds, but at places like Priory Lane, things that cannot be changed overnight.

Then there are increased costs associated with bigger crowds. More turnstiles to be opened, more programmes to be printed, more chips to be fried. Policing expenses can be astronomical. Many clubs at this level could feasibly lose money when a big team is in town.

In this situation the club's feelings can be mixed. And under FA regulations, clubs can no longer choose to switch their game to be played

Don't Take Anything For Granted

elsewhere, unless the police insist. So for many non League clubs, an away tie at a big club would be preferred. Clubs get a little under 50% of the gate for FA Cup ties so the benefits of an away trip are obvious. Getting a big team at home is not all that it is cracked up to be.

So there you have it. For us footy fans, we simply turn up. We pay our money, we watch the game, have a bit of a moan, a shout and (if we're lucky) a cheer. Then we go home. The club is always there and the volunteers are there long before we arrive and will be there long after we have left. And many of us (myself included) perhaps don't appreciate the detailed planning that goes into running a club and organising a match day, especially an FA Cup game against one of the big guns.

It is something we just take for granted.

Banana, Haddock And Black Pudding

The Eastbourne Borough v Weymouth game on Saturday is gearing up to be a cracking Cup tie. Neither set of fans are over confident about the result and both know it will be a difficult, close game. Any kind of predictions are proving hard to elicit. There promises to be a good atmosphere and I sense that a party mood will be prevalent. Eastbourne will have their drums and Weymouth fans will be wearing wigs for their journey along the South Coast.

Why wigs?

Well, back in 2005 Weymouth had a memorable day in the FA Cup First Round Proper away at Nottingham Forest where they held the League One side to a 1-1 draw. The Weymouth fans made a lasting impression after bringing a carnival atmosphere to the City Ground. The 1800 Weymouth fans on that day took with them a plethora of inflatables. After the success of the inflatables in 2005, the Dorset club have urged their fans to wear team coloured wigs (claret and blue) for the game this coming Saturday.

This story about the Weymouth inflatables reminded me of the craze in the late 1980s whereby supporters began to take inflatables to matches. I recall that Manchester City were one of the clubs to start this trend where the inflatable of choice was the banana. At West Ham it was the air-filled hammer. Bury had blown-up black puddings. And I never forget the inflatable haddock at Grimsby. I remember being trapped in a sea of Grimsby fans and large haddock which was all rather traumatising for me. So much so that I have never since been able face a plate of kedgeree without breaking into a cold sweat.

The inflatable craze was a great lift for the game in England at that time, which was still reeling from Heysel, hooliganism and the threat

Banana, Haddock And Black Pudding

of national identity cards. And I remember how it brought some good publicity back to the game. Football fans in our country do know how to party, and the FA Cup brings out the best, whether it's silly costumes, inflatables or wigs.

So this Saturday I'm looking forward to the drums and the wigs. Although I am relieved that there will be no haddock.

Thank Cod.

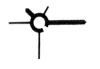

No Studs Please

What is happening to our country?

A school in Bexley, South East London, has banned children from wearing football boots for football training because they are deemed to be too dangerous. Bedonwell Primary School have said that children who attend any of the Charlton Athletic run football courses must wear plimsolls.

Good grief.

I really feel for the children these days. Kids can no longer play conkers because they are deemed to be "dangerous weapons". Two schools have banned them because of the risk to nut allergy sufferers. Children in Blackburn cannot do backstroke in the local swimming pool less they crash into someone. A school in Manchester has banned the wearing of knotted ties because of the "safety risk". The school now sells clip on ties. Traditional games such as British Bulldog, rounders and football are slowly disappearing from our playgrounds.

It's not only children affected. The Red Arrows have been banned from displaying at the 2012 Olympics in London because they are "too British" and we might offend other nations. Firefighters were told that they could not remove bunting in Ampthill, Bedfordshire because - wait for it - it is unsafe for them to use ladders. Camden Council have banned barbecues from summer festivals.

I really think we've lost the plot.

So no more football studs at Bedonwell Primary School. Despite the fact that trying to play football in plimsolls is far more dangerous for the children.

No Studs Please

Also in the news this week, England have been given the green light to bid for the 2018 World Cup. I really hope we get it; it will be a great spectacle. Footballers from all over the world competing for the biggest prize on our own doorstep.

The only problem is that they will all be asked to wear plimsolls.

My Glass Is Half Full

Is it just me, or are we hurtling towards Christmas at an alarming rate? Maybe it's my age, but time seems to pass quicker nowadays. On the eve of my second trip to Priory Lane, home of Eastbourne Borough, I can't quite believe that this season's FA Cup will, after tomorrow's game, be half complete. Or half remaining, depending on your view.

It feels like only yesterday that I went to the Extra Preliminary Round game between Chertsey Town and Wick, back in August. The kids were still off school, the days were long and some of the Chertsey players were still on the beach.

From the Extra Preliminary Round in August to the Final in May, there are a total of fourteen rounds. The seventh round will be played out this weekend. The games have come relatively thick and fast since August, one every two weeks (not counting replays). From now on though they start to spread out; three weeks between the First and Second Round Proper, a month between the Second and Third, and so on.

The rather sad thing for me is that many will see this weekend as the start of the FA Cup. Particularly the big media companies. The BBC and Sky TV now get in on the act. Sky TV will broadcast the Hereford United v Leeds United game tonight and the BBC will be showing Torquay United v Yeovil Town on Sunday. There will also be an FA Cup Match of the Day on Saturday evening. The draw for the First Round Proper was the first draw in this season's competition to attract live television coverage. All future round draws will be live. And if you read any of the mainstream newspapers this is when the FA Cup coverage really starts. You would be excused for believing that the previous six rounds didn't exist. The spotlight has just arrived.

But then this is not such a bad thing. The character of the competition has up to this stage has been enhanced somewhat by the relative anonymity. The small clubs, the tiny grounds, the local support, the sub-one hundred gates. Out of the eyes of mainstream media the FA Cup still sparkles and for me that is where it glitters brightest. It is more intimate. As an individual the early rounds allow you to get up close and personal. The only way to get any closer is to be playing.

But now here come the TV cameras, the bigger crowds, the greater recognition. The First Round Proper - even the title gives something away. And to be honest, my previous FA Cup viewing had only ever been from this stage of the competition. But this season it has been very different for me. I have learnt so much since August and I'll be the first to admit it has been a real eye-opener. There is still so much more the FA Cup will offer up this season and there is plenty to look forward to, but my involvement from the earliest knockings has seen my love affair with the FA Cup blossom.

The viewing gallery has suddenly got bigger. And my glass is, without doubt, only half full. It must be your round...

Eastbourne Borough 0 Weymouth 4
First Round Proper Saturday 10 November 2007
Attendance 2,711
Distance travelled 160 miles

Commemorative red balloons, 'Up for the Cup' t-shirts, extra turnstiles open - Eastbourne Borough were going to make the most of this day. And quite rightly so. This was a big occasion for the club. Only a few years ago Eastbourne's big Cup days came along courtesy of the Sussex Senior Cup. Following their impressive rise up the Leagues, Cup games in the FA Trophy and the FA Cup are becoming more common and here was an opportunity to advance to the FA Cup Second Round Proper for the first time in the club's short history.

This was also a big day for Sussex football; the first time that the county had been represented by four teams in the FA Cup First Round Proper. Eastbourne Borough were joined by Brighton & Hove Albion, Lewes and Horsham.

The Weymouth fans also played their part in the occasion; they travelled in numbers and as expected, were brightly attired. Fans from both clubs had been asked to arrive early to avoid the queues, and an impressive 2,711 people turned up. This gate must have surpassed all expectations. And did we have to queue! Myself and two friends (one Posh Mate and one Mackem) had to stand in line for almost everything. At the bar, at the turnstile, at the chip hatch and for the toilets. Not unlike me in the queue for the loo, Priory Lane was fit to burst. We witnessed another good Cup match in what were difficult, blustery conditions.

The first quarter of the game was really all Eastbourne Borough. They bossed possession and they played a lot of neat football. The diminutive Matt Crabb impressed the most, who started like a terrier but displayed some silky skills to boot. Most of the danger seemed to come from Crabb who had the desire and ability to run at speed with the ball, something all defenders dislike. The first real chance came on the 18th minute when the Weymouth goalkeeper John Stewart was forced to make a good save.

Game 9 Eastbourne Borough 0 Weymouth 4

Eastbourne maintained control throughout the half; for the final ten minutes of the half they tested the resolve of the referee's assistant with a number of long balls all of which were given offside. On the stroke of half-time Eastbourne Borough had an opportunity to break the deadlock with an unchallenged header from ten yards straight at the keeper.

In the second half, the home team began in the manner they had finished the first. Within minutes they had a shot cleared off the line. This seemed to stir both the Weymouth team and the Weymouth bench into action. The away team went straight up the other end and had an effort that was headed over for a corner. Whilst waiting for the corner to be taken, Weymouth threw on the tall substitute Jefferson Louis. With his first touch he headed in from the corner kick. One-nil to Weymouth after 52 minutes.

Weymouth had a couple of recognisable players in their team, namely Nick Crittenden and Paolo Vernazza. But it was this introduction of Louis that turned the game on its head for the Terras. From that point, Weymouth took complete control of the game. The extra height in attack for Weymouth caused problems in the Eastbourne rearguard and Weymouth had two more chances on 72 minutes to increase the lead. Eastbourne were now firmly on the back foot.

Crabb continued to show no fear with the ball at his feet, and he never gave up the chase, but you could feel the game ebbing away from Eastbourne. Around the hour mark the home team had had a penalty shout waived away by the referee; we were too far from the action to see whether it was a legitimate claim or not. That was Eastbourne's last chance to salvage anything and they spent the remainder of the game defending. Their resilience finally broke with three Weymouth goals in seven minutes, with a fine hat-trick from Stuart Beavon. The goals (80, 84 and 87 minutes) were all well worked and the Louis/Beavon partnership proved to be the difference between the two sides.

I actually missed the third goal (I was in the loo avoiding the final whistle queue) and Posh Mate missed the fourth. But I was able to see the goals on TV this morning; the first time I have been able to say that on this FA Cup run. It was a good-natured game, and only three yellow cards were produced. Although the referee's assistants seemed to come in for a degree of abuse from the home support and in particular, from Jason Tindall, the Weymouth manager. It takes a thick skin to run the line, especially with the crowd literally breathing down your neck.

Time for a cliché with which to summarise; this was a game of two halves. It really was. The first half belonged to the home side, who failed to capitalise. The second half belonged to Weymouth, who took their chances well. A thoroughly enjoyable clash. I think the scoreline flattered the away team a little, something echoed by the Weymouth fan I was standing next to. But credit to Weymouth for being the more clinical in the part of the pitch that matters.

We were treated to an impressive Sussex sunset as the light faded. Before the final whistle a couple of sorry-looking Eastbourne balloons drifted over the pitch and out towards the sea. This seemed to signify the end of the FA Cup dream for Eastbourne Borough. The club have much to look forward to this season, and promotion to the Blue Square Premier League is a fate in their own hands.

Of all the clubs that I have had contact with on this Cup run, Eastbourne Borough have been the most welcoming. The response from the club has been terrific, and I intend to keep in touch. I thank them for their hospitality and I wish them well. The baton now passes to Weymouth.

Draw for the Second Round Proper*: Cambridge United v Weymouth.*

A trip to Cambridgeshire next for me. Cambridge United v Weymouth on Saturday 1st December.

Doing this FA Cup run has meant that the draws take on a whole new meaning. If nothing else, they now (for me) pose a serious health risk.

Game 9 Eastbourne Borough 0 Weymouth 4

I was tired, drained and emotional after watching the live draw on Sunday. The home teams drawn out of the hat before the tie involving Weymouth were Oldham Athletic/Doncaster Rovers and Darlington/Northampton Town. The thought of long trips up north affected my ability to breath.

By the time Cambridge United v Weymouth had come out of the hat, I was barely conscious. It was a struggle to crawl to my PC, let alone write anything meaningful or incisive.

For me it's a pretty good draw really. Just over eighty miles (each way) for me to travel; nearer than Eastbourne. Another non League club and an all Blue Square Premier tie, so the guarantee of a non League club in the Third Round Proper. I'll get to meet up at the game with a friend I haven't seen in ages. The Cambridge United fans have already been good value. The Weymouth fans likewise... a pleasing draw all round.

The Staines Massive

Staines Town 1, Stockport County 1 (aet, Staines Town win 4-3 on penalties).

Stockport County may well be writing to the FA today to suggest that, in the FA Cup, the goals are just a tad bigger. The difference between success and failure (as my wife far too often reminds me) is just a matter of inches. Stockport had so many shots, so many near misses, that they really should now be contemplating a Second Round Proper date with Peterborough United.

But the beauty of the FA Cup was there for all to see at Wheatsheaf Park last night. As Dave Sargent, an estate agent, tucked away the winning penalty, the record crowd erupted with joy and spilled onto the pitch. This was another shock in a competition that continues to deliver.

On a bitterly cold night (I now have frostbite to go with the trench foot I acquired at the postponed game on Monday) I returned to Staines Town to witness the third attempt to complete this FA Cup First Round Proper replay. Just to clarify, this was an 'extra-curricular' FA Cup game for me, and not part of my road to Wembley journey. With Staines just down the road, I simply had to see this one.

I'm glad I did.

It was a typical Cup tie, the type I enjoy so much. A small ground packed to the rafters; non League part-timers versus League Two opposition; precarious TV camera gantries constructed especially for the game; a few non-paying customers scrambling over the wooden perimeter fence at half-time; young children watching the game from bedroom windows of adjacent houses. And a shock result to go with it!

The game finished 1-1 after Staines had led at half-time, with a powerful

The Staines Massive

header from Adrian Toppin following a corner. Stockport deservedly levelled on 78 minutes when Matty McNeil arrived unmarked at the far post to poke home. Against all expectations, Staines, who were visibly tiring and cramping up, held on through extra-time to take the game to penalties.

My 'man of the match' was the Staines keeper Shaun Allaway who put on a near faultless display to deny Stockport, and going into the shoot-out you felt that Allaway might make the difference. And he certainly did, with two wonderful penalty saves.

Cue Dave Sargent, cue the ecstatic scenes.

A thoroughly enjoyable evening.

So whilst I am up at Cambridge United on December 1st for the Weymouth tie, Staines Town of the Ryman Premier League will be hosting Cambridge rivals Peterborough United. Stockport County will have the Saturday off. Time to practice shooting on target perhaps?

Pass The Salt Please

I do like my salt. On chips. Crisps. Anchovies. Bovril. Bacon...crispy, salty bacon. Superb.

The bacon rolls at Cambridge United are famous. I'm looking forward to trying them out on Saturday, I've heard so much about them. I wonder if they sell Bovril as well? That would be too much too ask for...

One of my earliest memories as a child was of Bovril served with salt under the main stand at Maine Road, the then home of Manchester City. My father used to take me to the games, and although I always looked forward to the football, the big crowds and the great atmosphere, the thing I remember most about those visits in my youth was the cup of Bovril before the match. It was almost a ritual.

I would squeeze under the turnstiles hanging on to my Dad's coat tails, the turnstiles that were right there on the street opposite the two-up, two-down, terraced houses. Turnstiles that the locals could almost touch from their front doors. Once inside, I would follow down into the half-light of the voids below the stands, all concrete, metal supports and stairs leading off and up and to somewhere else. Down into a totally different world, a cavernous world that would be packed with expectant, excited supporters. For a six year old boy, it was a world of wonder and excitement. Through gaps in the stand you could glimpse a little of the pitch bathed in sunlight and the noise of the building crowd would roll in on the cold air and bounce off the walls. A promise of the excitement awaiting to unfold.

But first there was the pre-match ritual. A mass of blue and white scarves, flat caps and buttoned up overcoats, I remember it as always being cold on match days. But down here, the warmth was comforting. The warmth generated by the bodies. The steam from chattering breaths.

Pass The Salt Please

And the heat from the small food hatches. We, like everyone else down here, would be drawn to the the light and the hot smells tumbling out of these rectangular holes. We would immediately head for one of them and huddle round, a sea of legs. I would watch as my Dad ordered cups of boiling hot Bovril for him and his friends, then sip on them carefully as they flicked through the programme or discussed the skills of Summerbee, Bell or Tueart. I was in awe.

And I remember the first time my Dad bought a Bovril for me as if it was only yesterday. It tasted disgusting. But this was a seminal moment for me. It meant that I belonged. More than that, I had arrived. I was one of the crowd. I was a real football fan. The serving hatch would have a number of glass salt pots on the counter, and part of the Bovril ritual would be to sprinkle some salt into the black stuff. Barely tall enough to see the top of the counter, my Dad did this for me that first time. No question whether I wanted it or not. It came with the territory. I drank it all.

Now, I love the stuff. Bovril and salt. You can't beat it. I'm convinced that my taste for salt began there, in the bowels of Maine Road, as an awe-struck six year old boy. I know it's bad for you, but it is one of life's pleasures I refuse to give up on. Probably the only one, come to think of it.

But back to Cambridge United. I have been reminded by several people about Cambridge United and their bacon rolls. I recall that Colman's (of mustard fame) did a survey of the food served up at all ninety two Football League grounds, and Cambridge United came out top of the pile. Their bacon rolls received special mention. What surprises me most was that this survey was done back in 1998, almost ten years ago. The Cambridge club are still proud of this recognition; their bread with pork offerings even warrant a mention on their website.

So on Saturday, it would be remiss of me not to sample the bacon rolls. I'm licking my lips already. Pass the salt please.

If I Had A Little Money

Of course, the FA Cup is not only about the romance, the giant killings, the glory, the fans or the myriad of hopes and dreams up and down the country. There is also the money. The hard cash, the lolly, readies, greens, dough, moolah, bread, rhino, spondoolicks, motsa, beer tokens, boodle, dosh, poppy, wonga... whatever your name for it is, money will always play its part.

For the smaller clubs, this can be a pretty important part. Actually, a hugely significant part. For many clubs, a decent FA Cup run can be a saviour. For others, it can be the foundation for greater things.

On the eve of the FA Cup Second Round Proper both Cambridge United and Weymouth will have one eye on a potential money spinning game in the Third Round, the stage at which the big clubs enter the fray; and both clubs and fans will have that thought lurking somewhere in their minds. It is one of the ingredients that makes the FA Cup such an exciting dish.

The Second Round begins this evening when Horsham take on Swansea City, live on Sky TV. The Sussex club have had a fantastic Cup run already, disposing of Arundel, Bury Town, AFC Wimbledon, Chippenham Town and Maidenhead United. The run has netted them £37,000 from the FA Prize Fund. They will receive an additional £75,000 from the FA Broadcast Fund for tonight's Sky coverage. With Horsham planning to leave their Atspeed Stadium in the near future, some of this extra income will go towards the funding of their new ground.

This kind of FA Cup income swelling the coffers can make a real difference. Back in 2004, Exeter City of the Conference were in financial ruin, several million pounds in debt. They were managing to stay alive through the considerable efforts of the Exeter City Supporters Trust yet the future looked bleak. But then, Exeter City were pulled out of the velvet bag to play Manchester United in the Third Round of the FA Cup. The game at Old Trafford (in January 2005) finished 0-0 in front of over 67,000. This single match alone was worth £653,511 to Exeter. The replay at Exeter was televised which netted the Devon outfit a further £150,000. Their debts were settled in December 2005.

It is not only non League clubs, or clubs facing an uncertain future, that can benefit. In February 2006 Colchester United, at the time in the upper reaches of League One, were drawn away at Chelsea for a Fifth Round game. They had already seen off Sheffield United and Derby County. Their reward for reaching the last sixteen was £60,000 but with the Chelsea tie, they hit the jackpot. With TV coverage, gate receipts and merchandise sales, Colchester United netted close to £1 million from the competition. This income paid the wages for the squad for the remainder of the season which meant they were able to keep their squad together. They won promotion to the Championship and went on to have a successful first season (2006-07) at that level.

The money associated with a decent FA Cup run can, and will, make a difference to many clubs. For some, it may be the difference between survival or extinction. So good luck to all clubs this weekend, the Third Round awaits. Plus at least another £24,000 for getting there.

Cambridge United 1 Weymouth 0

Second Round Proper Saturday 1 December 2007
Attendance 4,552
Distance travelled 171 miles

They say that football is a universal language. It is the ice breaker at parties. It is the one thing most strangers have in common. In the corner of a small bar in Cambridgeshire yesterday, this was more than evident.

I travelled to the game with two good friends, Mackem and PB (surely you remember them from earlier games; how could you forget?). I arranged to meet another friend who lives in Cambridge; she has known me longer than I care to recall and therefore knows me far too well. Arrangements had also been made for me to be interviewed (about this mad venture) and we were to meet some budding young journalists, Dave, Dan and Gemma, who had travelled down from Lincoln for the game. What is the collective noun for a group of journalists - a scribe? Anyway, we all met in the Cambridge Supporters Club bar before the game and not one of us present knew everyone else. Not an uncommon event and not especially newsworthy. But within minutes we were all happily chatting as if we had known each other for some time.

This is one of the things that I enjoy about football. We all had one single thing in common - the love of this beautiful game. The clubs supported around the table ranged from Cambridge United to QPR to Blackburn and to Liverpool. But we all had footy experiences to share, the same (old) jokes about other teams, fond memories of games gone by, expectations of games to come. This was more than me being interviewed. It was a group of strangers having a good old chin-wag about blokes who kick balls.

If I were to be brutally honest, that hour or so in the bar before the game was probably the highlight of the day. Dave, Dan and Gemma were excellent hosts. The game itself was pretty poor. In defence of both sets of players, the windy conditions prevented any sort of decent, flowing football. This was more like a bun fight in a gale. Not pretty.

81

Game 10 Cambridge United 1 Weymouth 0

The kick-off was delayed for fifteen minutes as the crowds struggled into the Abbey Stadium. The official attendance was 4,552, the biggest gate on my journey so far. My last visit to this ground must have been around ten years ago, and there has been some development since then. The majority of the ground still had a bit of a run down feel to it; ageing stands and rusting metalwork. But the stand that housed the Weymouth fans was rather impressive; this South Stand positively gleamed in comparison to the rest of the ground, bright amber with bold black 'CUFC' lettering. Weymouth support seemed quite low, and the stand dwarfed the away contingent. It was, however, nice to see a fair proportion of the ground still terraced, something which is sadly disappearing from our game.

As for the match itself, I'm afraid there is not an awful lot to report. The wind had the upper hand. The most entertaining aspect of the first half was the inability of the Weymouth goalkeeper, Jason Matthews, to kick anywhere other than into touch to his left. It became increasingly comical to watch his failed attempts, his clearances regularly hoisted upon the wind and blown into the Main Stand. The poor guy was struggling and the Cambridge fans behind his goal were less than sympathetic. On one occasion he contrived to slice a dead ball in to touch on the opposite side which reduced the home support to fits of laughter.

Cambridge started the strongest and had a few decent chances in the first few minutes. Early doors Cambridge won a free kick and Gavin Hoyte forced a fantastic save from the Weymouth keeper. The home team had three reasonable chances in the first fifteen minutes all of which were turned away by the visiting goalie. Along with his battle with the wind, Matthews was fast becoming the centre of attention in the first half. The Cambridge fans began to chant "we want eight" in reference to their 7-0 drubbing of Weymouth earlier this year.

Then, rather fortuitously, Cambridge United scored from a penalty on twenty six minutes. Scott Rendell broke into the area on the angle and cut across his marker. There was the slightest of contact and Rendell went down. A bit too easily for me, but from where the referee was

Game 10 Cambridge United 1 Weymouth 0

standing there was little choice for the man in the middle. Rendell brushed himself down to tuck the penalty away with aplomb. One-nil to the hosts at half-time.

In the second half, it was Cambridge's turn to battle with the elements and to be fair, as the game progressed, Weymouth looked the more likely to score. The second half was ever so scrappy and became totally, and painfully, bogged down in midfield. The Cambridge drummer (yet another game with a percussionist!) tried his hardest to drum up some sort of atmosphere. The rhythmic beat seemed to animate the crowd, but this was more likely a desperate attempt to combat the falling temperature. It was now so cold that body parts were starting to numb. I had by now lost all feeling below my waist and any my efforts to move in time with the beat were simply pathetic; think of a pissed Pinocchio and you will get the picture.

One of my friends commented on how little happened in the second half yet without the usual associated feeling that the game was dragging. I put it down to the body shutting down the brain. Hypothermia in a nutshell. I even thought I saw Santa Claus in amongst the Weymouth fans.

But then, with quarter of an hour to go, Weymouth realised they had to commit more men forward if they were to stay in the competition and it was in this final period that they created most of their chances. Their pressure culminated with a corner in the dying minutes from Anton Robinson which floated onto the bar, and bounced out for a goal kick. And with this last chance, Weymouth were blown out of the FA Cup.

A poor performance from Cambridge United, and they stumbled through to the Third Round. But a win is a win, one that their manager Jimmy Quinn described as "ugly". I'm afraid I can't disagree.

So my tenth game ended with a single goal separating the teams, and Cambridge United take over as the team to follow. Even though the

Game 10 Cambridge United 1 Weymouth 0

game was far from a classic - the bacon rolls had even failed to live up to expectations - it had been another enjoyable day out.

For me, the chance to meet new acquaintances was the high point of the day. With hindsight, maybe we should have stayed in the bar. As always though, this is much easier said than done.

Draw for Third Round Proper: Wolverhampton Wanderers v Cambridge United.

The draw for the Third Round Proper of this season's FA Cup was made yesterday at Soho Square. By the time Cambridge United's number was pulled out of the hat, there weren't that many teams left. But tie number twenty seven (out of thirty two) means that it is a trip off to Molineux for me in January, a ground I last visited in the early 1980s. Lots of amber and black to look forward to.

The Story That Never Was

The Internet. What a marvellous thing, the 'invention' of our time. The power of instant communication, information available at the click of a mouse, making a mockery of physical distance at the touch of a button.

My FA Cup journey owes much to the Internet; it has basically made my life so much easier. Finding information about the competition format, the dates of games (and replays), about tickets, ground locations, travel. It allows for immediate and rapid communication with the clubs and their fans. In fact everything connected with my road towards the Final. All this has been done from the comfort of the spare room.

Not to mention this blog. In equal measure I have enjoyed going to the games, meeting new people and writing about it all. As I have alluded to a few times already, the response I have had to this blog, since my first post on 24th August, has shocked me. And it continues to do so, daily. As I write this post this evening, there have so far been 13,071 page views in 7,027 different visits to the blog. This is from 3,087 unique visitors in 53 different countries.

Now, in Internet terms, not huge figures, but for something that started out as a stroll down the lane to watch Chertsey Town on a cool August summer evening, these stats never cease to surprise.

Of course, without the accessibility that the Internet creates, none of this would have been possible. The clubs along my journey have assisted with the access. Links on the home pages of the websites of Sittingbourne, Dartford, Eastbourne Borough and (most recently) Cambridge United have helped. Add to that mention of the site in a number of match day programmes, non League football publications and over match tannoys, and the fingers of the web are encouraged to spread further and wider and deeper. But the Internet can also be a perilous place, especially when the information you find is of dubious quality or questionable calibre.

On the way into work today I was amazed to hear a radio newsreader declare that there had been "a mistake" with the FA Cup draw on Sunday. The draw for the Third Round Proper. The one that paired Cambridge United with Wolverhampton Wanderers. This 'news' even made some of today's newspapers. You could probably understand my reaction. What on earth is going on? Would the draw have to be done again? Maybe I'm not off to Wolves after all? Probably Trevor Brooking's fault (again).

As it turned out, this was the story that never was. There was no mistake, no error, no blunder. A conspiracy theory of sorts, that had broken on the World Wide Web early on Tuesday and had spread like wildfire across the ether to make big news within a matter of hours. The "mistake" reported was that the number 25 ball had been drawn out of the bowl but the number 24 read aloud instead. If this indeed had happened, it would have meant that Manchester United should be playing Bristol City instead of Aston Villa.

But photographs and video stills of the draw proved that there had been no mistake. The number 24 ball had been pulled out and read out. End of.

But it just goes to show how powerful the Internet can be, something that the conspiracy theorists can use to great effect. And often do. Many things are written on the Internet that people believe and over time are perceived as fact or, at best, written into folklore. The 9/11 conspiracy theory is probably the most notable example. Of course, this is nothing new; the Internet alone is not to blame. Storytelling as a form of communication has been in existence since man could stand unaided on two legs, and stories have always been passed from generation to generation. The mere passing of time allows for the real facts to be diluted and the (usually more interesting or newsworthy) fiction to be elaborated. The difference with the Internet is that the time element is

The Story That Never Was

condensed - for thousands of years read days, for hundreds of years, read minutes. And the fact that we can view something 'in print' on a screen fools us into thinking that what we are reading is true.

We can all be easily fooled. Personally, I blame the bloggers. Especially the idiots who write about football...

Why?

I need to get this off my chest. It is something that annoys me this time every year. Each and every year it's the same. Please bear with me, this won't take long.

In an early post, I bemoaned the fact that, as the FA Cup progresses through the rounds, it will inevitably lose some of the 'romance' as smaller clubs and the non League outfits fall by the wayside. One of my comments (back in early November) was this:

"the BBC always chose to televise a dull all-Premier League tie in the Third Round".

And, low and behold, the BBC's choice for the first live game of the Third Round Proper is Aston Villa v Manchester United.

Now, don't get me wrong, I have nothing against either club. Both are playing good football this season, and it should be a most entertaining game. But why? Why, BBC, why?

The FA Cup has so much to offer. The real appeal, surely, is the prospect of a team punching above their weight. Villa v United just doesn't do that for me. It doesn't scream out 'FA Cup' to me, not just yet anyway. It may do if it were a Semi-Final tie, but not at this stage of the competition.

The BBC will position themselves well to defend this selection. They will argue based on the amount of support there is for both clubs. But don't we already see enough of these teams on TV? Match of the Day (or Match of the Day 2) every week shows, as a minimum, their goals. If not, then highlights. Both feature heavily in Sky live games. And now also on Setanta. Not too mention ITV's coverage of United's Champions League games.

Why?

As a child, the FA Cup Final on TV was the only live game that you could watch from the comfort of the living room. It was the occasion of the season, the highlight of the football calendar. It was the rarest of treats. FA Cup Final day viewing would start around nine or ten o'clock on the Saturday morning; I would fight, with my brother and friends, for the best vantage point on the sofa, from a very early hour. And sit mesmerised in the same position, all day. For one simple reason; a live game on TV was a novelty. It didn't really matter who was playing.

Now, we are spoilt for choice. I hate to say this, but for me the FA Cup Final as a televisual spectacle has lost that attraction that it once held. It may still be a big fish, but it has been engulfed in a big pond with many other big fish to swim against.

How many times have Villa met United in the FA Cup? This will be the fourth time in seven seasons, all in the Third Round Proper. And it is not the first time the BBC have chosen the exact same tie to beam into our front rooms.

So go on BBC, be brave. There are so many interesting Third Round games that could be screened instead. Games that really do scream 'FA Cup' at me. OK, BBC will also be screening Burnley v Arsenal, and Stoke City v Newcastle United, which isn't too bad. But what is wrong with getting Havant & Waterlooville on the box instead? It would be great for the club. Or Bury at Norwich City? Colchester United v Peterborough United? Or (dare I say it) Cambridge United at Wolves? The later rounds will no doubt be packed with all Premiership ties, so why not wait until then?

This is why there is a commonly held view that the FA Cup has lost some of its old sparkle and shine. If the BBC keep offering up live matches that involve clubs that the armchair fans are used to watching week in, week out, then those same fans become immune to them.

Let's have a bit of variety, and a bit of imagination.

Why?

Bring back the romance! Give the smaller clubs a little limelight! Isn't that what the FA Cup is all about? Or am I totally missing the point? I know the BBC will never change, and each season I will find myself asking the same question.

Why?

An Evening At The Emirates

My old man used to say: "If that's your Nan at the door, tell her I'm out."

There are some things in life you cannot avoid, and one of them is the lure of the big games. A diversion from the FA Cup saw me down at the Emirates Stadium, on Wednesday evening, to take in the Champions League fixture between Arsenal and FC Steaua Bucureşti.

One of the joys of this FA Cup journey has been experiencing football at all levels and all standards, and turning up at games in the lower echelons has been most rewarding. But I could not spurn the opportunity to go to a big game; a big club, big stars, big crowd, big occasion. Most of my football as a youth was watching games in the top flight of English football, and I have never lost that thrill or the excitement of being part of a big match atmosphere. Old Trafford, Anfield, Elland Road, Maine Road, Goodison Park. Those were the theatres of my formative years.

The adrenalin rush experienced from the power and noise of a huge crowd is one of life's greatest feelings. Now and then I need a fix.

I had been looking forward to this trip for quite some time. It isn't easy getting tickets for a match at Arsenal's new ground. It nearly always sells out. There is a seriously long waiting list for season tickets, and if you are not a season ticket holder you need to be a club member before you can buy entrance. A friend holds club membership and he very kindly purchased a ticket for me courtesy of his wife's membership card. From now on you can call me Diana.

I knew this game was going to be all about contrasts in comparison to my FA Cup games this season, and it certainly goes without saying that this would be a totally different experience. Alwyns Lane, Bourne Park,

An Evening At The Emirates

Krooner Park. Now for the Emirates Stadium. But the most striking contrast hit me within a few minutes of stepping out of Arsenal tube station. It was the old and the new.

Turn left out of the tube and you are in amongst the terraced streets close to the old Highbury stadium. The facade of the old stadium remains, visible down a side street, in all its glory. Flats are being built where the turf used to be. But all down here, along Gillespie Road, it was a hive of activity. The street was flanked with small stalls and wooden huts, almost like an old evening market. The goods on sale included Arsenal memorabilia (shirts, scarves, badges), old programmes, refreshments (hot dogs, burgers, etc.) and even a sweet stall. Further down the street the corner chippy was doing a roaring trade; a delicious bag of chips for a quid (plenty of salt). The lights from all the stalls illuminated the street and the house gardens, and the place was all steam and smells. This matchday scene has no doubt been repeated for decades. This was the old.

Then back down Gillespie Road, around the corner and there was the new. Wallop, it knocked your senses for six. The contrast could not have been more striking. The Emirates is a huge, spaceship like structure, all silver and neon and shiny. Immense, it dominates its surroundings. It is an impressive sight. The stadium has been designed well, and it is evident that this is a ground built as much for the comfort of the fans as anything else. Huge, open concourses; plenty of facilities (toilets, food and drink points). No queues. Great views with no obstructions from any part of the ground. And the seats. I loved the seats. Majestically large, acres of leg room and all with soft padding - certainly a football first for me. Every single seat in the stadium is the same - we were not located in a particularly ostentatious part of the ground which provided extra-comfy specially padded seats. This was the norm.

But you pay for the privilege. If you want to watch Arsenal at home, be prepared to shell out anything upward of £45. Over £60 for the bigger games.

An Evening At The Emirates

I was quite taken by the seats at the Emirates. The following day, I found myself boring a few friends about the quality seating. I didn't realise that my wife was stood behind me whilst I was in full flow. I ended by saying that "it was more comfortable than watching a game in our front room" at which point my wife made her presence known. Oops. My wife is now wondering if we ought to buy a new sofa. I can tell her now; it won't be delivered before Christmas.

The match itself however was a tad lame. Played out on a velvety turf, Arsenal cruised their way to half-time, scoring two goals and deserving more. They fielded a youthful team - no Fabregas, Gallas, Hleb or Adebayor. Arsenal had already qualified for the knockout stages of the Champions League. They were playing for top spot in the group (and, arguably, a more favourable draw) but that outcome relied on Sevilla failing to win at Sparta Prague. In the second half, Arsenal took their foot off the gas. They squandered midfield superiority to a Steaua team that seemed to want it more. The Romanian side pulled one back and looked increasingly likely to grab a draw. Arsenal however hung on to win 2-1. Elsewhere, Sevilla got the result they needed which meant Arsenal finished as group runners-up.

I must admit that I was disappointed with the atmosphere inside the Emirates Stadium. It did not live up to expectations. Partly, I guess, to do with the opposition and the sense of inevitability surrounding the game. The 59,786 crowd were rather subdued. However, when Chelsea and Manchester United visit, I'm sure the atmosphere would crank up.

I couldn't help thinking of the bigger stadiums I used to go to in my youth, with their packed terraces. The thrill of being part of a huge, standing crowd swaying and singing as one, the rush of blood as a goal went in. It was exhilarating. Those days are now firmly in the past. The old has been replaced by the new, and the experience that is watching football continues to change. It saddens me a little.

But boy, I did like those seats.

A View From A Terrace

The team that currently has the misfortune of my company in this season's FA Cup is Cambridge United. I say misfortune, as I don't think I bring much luck. I have only seen one team (Dartford) progress further than two rounds. The law of averages suggests that my trip to Wolverhampton in January may witness Cambridge United's exit from the competition. If this proves to be the case, then I apologise now to the supporters from Cambridgeshire.

As for Cambridgeshire, things are looking rather rosy for the county as far as football is concerned. United are riding high in the Blue Square Premier. They have also been joined in that League this season by Histon, for the first time in their history; the highest level that Histon have ever played football at. Cambridge City are one level lower, holding their own in the Blue Square South. Before United's New Year trip to the Black Country they have a very important League double header against Histon over the Christmas period. It is going to be an exciting festive period for football fans in the city and bragging rights for the remainder of the season will be there for the taking.

However, Cambridge United's biggest rivals are county neighbours Peterborough United. 'The Posh' are also having a good season; they are challenging for automatic promotion from League Two. Along with Cambridge United, they are also through to the Third Round of the FA Cup and face an away game against Championship opposition (Colchester United). To say that Cambridge United and Peterborough United are rivals is like saying that Arsene Wenger and Sir Alex Ferguson don't get on much. The word 'intense' springs to mind.

So on Saturday I took another trip to Cambridgeshire, this time to see the rivals across the fens. Having been to Arsenal midweek, I knew that this was going to be an experience of our beautiful game from yet

A View From A Terrace

another, quite different, perspective. The Posh were hosting Milton Keynes Dons.

At the start of the day the visitors were top of the League with Peterborough four points behind in second. The game had been greatly anticipated for a number of weeks, and the Peterborough club had pulled out all stops to promote the clash. This paid off; 10,351 turned out for the game, more than double their season's average. And with it, they brought an absolutely cracking, almost electric, atmosphere. Outside the ground long before kick-off, one could sense that the atmosphere had been charged and cranked up over a number of days to the point that it was starting to crackle before turnstiles began to turn. Expectations in the city were high.

The game itself was a very good advert for football in League Two. For the neutral, it had just about everything; three good goals, two teams at the top of their game, numerous chances for both sides, plenty of goalmouth action, some bizarre referring decisions, a sending off, and a Partridge in a pear tree (not really).

The home side just about edged the first half, with a glorious effort from Charlie Lee striking the bar after fifteen minutes. The three goals arrived in the second half. In a bizarre ten minute period the Peterborough defence went totally absent, conceding two goals which could quite easily have been five or six; Gallen (47) and Andrews (57) making the most of gaping holes at the back. The home team should have been dead and buried.

But in an almost Cup-like contest, Peterborough threw everything at the visitors in an attempt to purloin something from the game. Mclean pulled one back with a quarter of an hour remaining and an unlikely comeback looked feasible when Diallo was dismissed for the Dons on 78 minutes. In a barn-storming finish, MK Dons did just about enough to hang on for a deserved 2-1 victory. A delighted Paul Ince (Dons) and a dejected Darren Ferguson (Posh).

A View From A Terrace

What a great game. Without any hesitation I can say that this was a much better game than the one at the Emirates on Wednesday. But even more notably, the atmosphere at London Road eclipsed that I experienced in the spanking new stadium in North London.

Here were two teams that had everything to play for. Here were two teams whose levels of expectations, compared to Arsenal, are relatively lower. The battle for League Two supremacy for these two teams means just as much as Champions League success means for Arsenal. And here were two teams that ran themselves into the ground and in doing so served up a highly entertaining game for a crowd who had been wound up to the point of bursting.

But the best bit? I witnessed all of this stood on the steps of a terrace. Grand!

The road starts here - Alwyns Lane, home of Chertsey Town FC.

Dartford supporters look forward to their First Qualifying Round tie against Sittingbourne, but The Darts required a replay to get through.

Bromley supporters fly the flag ahead of their Kentish derby (or is it?) against Dartford in the Third Qualifying Round, but programme sales aren't exactly brisk at Hayes Lane.

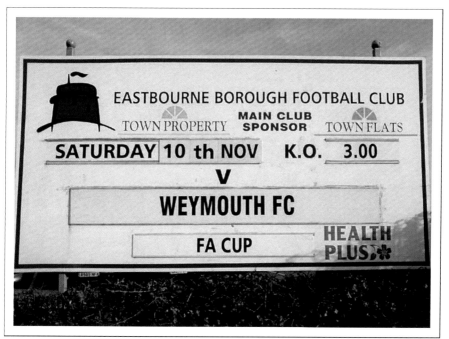

The First Round Proper throws up an all-South Coast tie as Eastbourne Borough welcome Weymouth to Priory Lane.

Visiting Weymouth fans sport an assortment of 'fashionable headgear' for their visit. Apparently it's all the rage in Dorset.

Cambridge United supporters pay on the day as The U's see off Blue Square Premier rivals Weymouth in their Second Round Proper tie.

An alternative 'Watford Gap' at Vicarage Road; whilst The Riverside Stadium prepares to welcome Cardiff City.

Middlesbrough fans with an eye on Wembley prior to their Sixth Round tie against Cardiff City. The youngster on the right appears to already know what the outcome will be.

A young Bluebird at Wembley, whilst other Cardiff fans refuse to subscribe to the stereotypical image the English have of the Welsh and sheep!

Cardiff fans give a rousing rendition of 'Men of Harlech' before kick-off but at full-time it is the Portmouth fans who have most to sing about.

The £1 Deal

There's no such thing as a free lunch.

The FA are offering children the opportunity to watch FA Cup games in the Third Round for £1. When I first read about this last week, my initial reaction was positive. A noble effort to get more kids along to games and what better games than the ones the FA Cup has to offer. To use the FA's own words:

"...to encourage parents to introduce their children to the magic and excitement of the FA Cup – for just £1 a ticket".

Great. I know many clubs have done this for non-Cup games as well, and it is to be applauded. Dartford charged only £1 for the football fans of the future for their Second Qualifying Round tie against Camberley Town back in September. And my son loved it (as you may recall).

But hold on a minute. This £1 deal applies to only six of the thirty two ties:

Blackburn Rovers v Coventry City
Bolton Wanderers v Sheffield United
Huddersfield Town v Birmingham City
Plymouth Argyle v Hull City
Sunderland v Wigan Athletic
Wolverhampton Wanderers v Cambridge United

Why is that then?

Well, the FA say that they have made that selection based on a fair mix of geographical location and of ties involving teams from a variety of different Leagues. Fair enough, most Leagues are represented in that

The £1 Deal

selection; Premiership (5 teams), Championship (5), League One (1) and Blue Square Premier (1). But geographical location? Four of the six ties are up north - two in the North West, one in the North East and one in Yorkshire. Throw in a couple more from the South West and the Midlands, and that is not what I'd call an even geographical distribution.

No games from London. No games from the South East.

But then, I shouldn't be surprised. Looking at those six games selected, with the possible exception of Sunderland, none will be sold out to capacity. On the day, there will be empty seats in most of those stadiums, including my venue of fate, Molineux. It comes as no surprise that some of the bigger clubs are not partaking. I would have thought Chelsea v QPR would have been an ideal choice; an opportunity to get kids along to see a team that continues to price many people out of the market. Arsenal, Chelsea, Liverpool and Manchester United are also noticeable by their absence.

So the real deal slogan should be "bring your child for £1, with a full paying adult, so that we can get some bums on those otherwise empty seats and, as a result, makes for a financially better deal for the clubs". Doesn't really roll off the tongue, does it?

Am I'm being too cynical? Probably. Go on; take your kids along to a game that weekend. They'll love it. But you'll still have to buy them lunch.

Man 'flu

Pounding head. Tight chest. Aching limbs. Sore throat. Bunged up nose. I thought I had avoided this winter's bout of lurgy. Both my nieces were full of it over Christmas, my wife brought it back home with us for New Year and now it's my turn.

I feel as rough as anything and have been in bed with nothing more than a high temperature and the odd shot of 'Night Nurse' for two days now.

My trip up to the Midlands for the Wolves v Cambridge United game is now in jeopardy. This could be, to date, the greatest risk to the whole venture. You may recall that I almost missed a trip to Dartford in an early Qualifying Round when my wife badly damaged her ankle. I made that journey, laden with guilt.

Tonight I will need a good, restful sleep. And a miraculous recovery. If I do make the trip, it won't be guilt I'll be full of but something far less pleasant.

My road to Wembley could all end, here and now, amongst a flurry of tissues.

Wolverhampton Wanderers 2 Cambridge United 1
Third Round Proper Saturday 5 January 2008
Attendance 15,340
Distance travelled 272 miles

In the end I could not let a bout of illness prevent me from going to this game, although my body was trying its hardest to tell me otherwise. My wife could not understand my desire to leave the warmth of the house and it was futile to even attempt to explain.

On this, we agreed to disagree.

I doubt if I would have made it to the game if it hadn't been for the support of my mates. As determined as I was that I should continue this venture, they offered to share the driving - I was certainly in no fit (nor legal) state to drive - and for that I am most appreciative. I was joined once again by Mackem and PB (who did most of the driving) and a road to Wembley virgin, Captain Beaky (who did some of the driving early on but mysteriously succumbed to some kind of nasal virus halfway up the M40). PB and Mackem have shared a good portion of this venture with me and fully understood that non-attendance at the game was simply not an option.

Attending a game of football drugged to the eyeballs is a rather peculiar experience, something I don't recall ever having done before. It was almost like watching the match from inside a bubble. An almost total detachment from reality. All my senses were numbed. My taste buds were shot to an extent that the pre-match Meat & Potato pie could have contained Pedigree Chum for all I knew, although I must say my friends approved of the Chicken Balti offerings. My hearing was muffled which wasn't such a bad thing as we were sat in front of a small group of 'kids for a quid' spectators who were keen to make the most of their free miniature horns. I was thankfully quite immune to their high pitch tooting.

Although at times I wondered if I was the only one on the medication. As the Wolves mascots left the pitch just prior to kick-off, I was drawn

Game 11 Wolverhampton Wanderers 2 Cambridge United 1

into a bizarre conversation between PB and Captain Beaky, who were sat either side of me. One of the mascots was evidently male (outfitted in trousers) whilst the other was female (skirt). PB and Captain Beaky quickly agreed that they were the strangest looking 'bears' they had ever seen. Bears! We were about to watch Wolves and these mascots had big pointy ears (all the better to hear with), big pointy noses (all the better to smell with) and big pointy teeth (all the better to eat you up with). Good grief! It was at that moment I realised that there was an advantage in being totally desensitised.

For the first time in this FA Cup run, I felt a real detachment from the actual game and from the host club, Wolves. Prior to the match, I had had no contact with club officials. There was no mention in the match day programme. No tannoy announcing my presence. I was simply one of 15,340 at the game. This was also the first time that we had no choice as to how we watched the game. We had to sit and stay in the same seat for the duration. Our seats, although offering a good view of proceedings, were physically quite removed from the pitch. The close involvement with club and game that I had become accustomed to on this run had suddenly, and quite abruptly, come to an end. I had anticipated this happening at some stage, but I was still not prepared for it. I'm now not sure if that feeling of involvement will ever return in this season's FA Cup.

As for the game, it was an enjoyable ninety minutes of Cup action, and for a not insignificant time it looked as if we were going to witness an FA Cup shock.

Cambridge brought with them an excellent following and, if anyone still questions the beauty of the FA Cup and what it means to fans, I would simply point doubters in the direction of the travelling support from Cambridgeshire yesterday. Over 4,000 United supporters occupied the whole of the Steve Bull lower stand and part of the Jack Harris stand; their vocal support for their team was one of the highlights of the day and a credit to non League football. As the team emerged onto the

Game 11   Wolverhampton Wanderers 2   Cambridge United 1

pitch, a barrage of tiny pieces of yellow paper was cast into the air for a magnificent paper storm reception. The Cambridge fans had actually spent hours shredding numerous copies of the 'Yellow Pages' prior to the game. Well worth the effort. Boca Juniors eat your heart out.

By contrast, the Wolves fans were rather muted. The attendance was well below average. They are having a tough time at the moment, and for long periods of the match Mick McCarthy did a very passable impression of an awfully lonely man in his technical area.

The hosts almost scored within the first minute of the game when Jay Boothroyd found space only for his weak effort to be blocked by Albrighton. Within minutes Cambridge had their first chance when Convery forced a save out of Wayne Hennessey in the Wolves goal. These two early exchanges set the pattern for the remainder of an entertaining first half. Both sides had a number of reasonable chances, only for poor finishing to stifle any chance of reward. Gibson and Ward for Wolves should have scored openers but tame shots straight at the United keeper quickly became the order of the day.

Then just before half-time, a breakthrough came for Cambridge United with a soft penalty decision. The ball appeared to strike the arm of Wolves defender Neill Collins but the referee wasted no time in pointing to the spot. Scott Rendell, as he had done in the previous round of this competition, comfortably converted to send the travelling support into mass frenzy. 1-0 to the visitors after forty two minutes and a Cup shock appeared to be taking shape.

Into the second half and one could sense the agitation and frustration amongst the home support. McCarthy continued to prowl from his controlled zone, but his Wolves, in all honesty, did not have any bite. Michael Gray (three England caps) was awful with his distribution. Boothroyd was both greedy and wasteful in equal measure. Things only really began to turn in the home team's favour with a couple of substitutions. Freddie Eastwood's arrival lifted the crowd and possession

Game 11 Wolverhampton Wanderers 2 Cambridge United 1

swung in favour of the men in black and gold. But this merely led to more wasted chances with Ward (again) and Eastwood guilty of missing the target. On the hour McCarthy brought on local favourite Michael Kightly; within nine minutes of his arrival he had scored to level the game, sweetly turning in a cross by Matt Jarvis. And then in the dying minutes of the game Kightly provided the centre which was headed into the back of the net by a (no doubt) relieved Neill Collins. Wolves sneak into the next round.

To sum up the game I think Cambridge were a tad unlucky not to get another bite at the cherry. Wolves were simply very poor at times and there were spells in the game when one would have been excused for thinking that both teams played their League football at comparable levels. McCarthy's substitutions appeared to have worked but will this cut any slack with an increasingly unhappy home support? Would a draw have been a fairer result? Perhaps, but that may well be my FA Cup heart ruling my head.

Talking of my head, it still feels as thick and as heavy as a bucket of mushy peas. My wife thinks I have more than a simple cold and I'm off to the docs tomorrow to get checked out. As all married men know, but rarely admit, the missus is always right. I won't be surprised if the diagnosis is Cup fever.

Draw for the Fourth Round Proper: Watford v Wolverhampton Wanderers.

First things first. My wife was right. I've returned from an early appointment with my GP who sent me away with antibiotics, a five day sick note and a flea in my ear about travelling over 270 miles to watch football with a respiratory infection. I've already decided that my epitaph will read "I told you I was ill".

Wolverhampton Wanderers now take up the torch in my FA Cup marathon and they have a tough trip to fellow Championship side Watford. For me, a short hop around the M25, assuming I can get tickets. A pretty

Game 11 Wolverhampton Wanderers 2 Cambridge United 1

reasonable draw. In the meantime, I'll carry on taking the tablets.

So it is goodbye to Cambridge United. What's more, for me, it is goodbye to non League football in this season's competition; short of a miracle involving Havant & Waterlooville getting into the next round at the expense of first Swansea City and then either Luton Town or Liverpool. The cord to the non League scene, born on that cool summer's evening back in August down at the end of my lane, has finally been severed. After 11 games and 138 days and 1350 miles of tarmacadam.

731 clubs registered to take part in this season's FA Cup, and come the weekend of the 25th and 26th January for the Fourth Round Proper this number will have been whittled down to just thirty two. Looking at that list of original entries, it starts with Abbey Hey and ends with Yorkshire Amateur. Wolverhampton Wanderers and Watford are snugly positioned toward the end of the list amongst teams such as Wick and Weymouth (seen them), Whitehawk and Wootton Blue Cross (wish I had seen them) and Wembley (hoping to see it).

We are now down to the last sixteen ties.

Chicken And Egg

I hope I've got this wrong. Maybe I've been too quick to pass judgement. Maybe someone is winding me up. I am quite gullible. But I'm starting to question Watford's approach to their paying customers.

It all started when the Fourth Round draw was made that paired Wolves with Watford. As you'd expect, one of the first things I did was to make some enquiries about the game; whether it will be an all-ticket affair and how I could go about getting a ticket. I contacted the club, and in all honesty they were extremely responsive. I got the standard "ticket details will be announced in due course" reply; Watford have since announced that tickets will go on sale to Season Ticket Holders only. However, tickets will not go on general sale until Monday 21st January, a matter of days before the game.

Further digging (mainly with the Watford fans) made me aware of a 'database' that Watford FC run for ticket allocation. Now, this is the bit I may have got wrong, but I have been told by several fans that I need to be on this database before I can buy tickets. Stories have been recounted of fans being turned away on match days because, whilst trying to buy tickets, it transpired that they were not on this database. This happened at a recent game (Watford v Crystal Palace in the last round of the FA Cup) where the final attendance was only 10,480, several thousand short of capacity. Surely this can't be true. Can it? Why turn away good business? Why refuse permission to fans that had turned up and were ready to pay, had the cash in their hands? Why do this when the ground was only half full? Or, more pertinently, half empty?

I checked with the club, and yes, there is a database which you need to be on before you can buy tickets. I asked how you get on the database? The answer? "After you have bought tickets, your details are put on the database". Come again?

Chicken And Egg

Talk about chicken and egg. I was told to call back on Monday 21st January...

Having slept on this, I had decided that this simply was a misunderstanding and, come the day of reckoning, I would have no problems buying tickets over the phone. But then only today I heard this story about Watford FC.

A Watford fan had arranged a massive outing to watch a Watford game; he had just over 315 children and adults in his party. He booked this with the club some time ago, and managed to get discount for party size. The discounted costs averaged £20 for an adult and £8 for a child. Some time after those arrangements were made, Watford then announced that ticket prices for the game in question would actually be reduced. The new prices for the game were £10 for an adult and only £1 for the kids. Understandably, Watford would charge this huge party the new prices, saving the organiser something in the region of £2,750. Wouldn't they?

Well, no. They wouldn't. In what has become a PR disaster, Watford are refusing to back down on this. They insist that the original prices be charged. In the words of the party organiser: "so what started as a good opportunity for WFC to encourage some young new fans is turning into something a little distasteful - I certainly wouldn't do it again and we take hundreds every year to at least one match".

Oh dear. Can someone tell me what is going on down at Watford?

So it maybe is a little naive of me to think I'll have no problems getting tickets for the Wolves game, even though early indications suggest it will not be sold out. I am prepared to be proven wrong and I'm keen to give Watford FC the benefit of the doubt. However, it really could be a chicken and egg situation with this database.

It all sounds a bit fowl to me.

The Dream Had Become Reality

"The dream had become reality".

These are the words of Havant & Waterlooville manager Shaun Gale after watching his side's sensational 4-2 victory over Swansea City in the FA Cup on Wednesday evening.

I don't think "sensational" is too strong a word to use. Up for grabs was not only a nice, tidy sum of prize money but a trip to Liverpool in the Fourth Round. Swansea would have wanted that reward just as much as Havant & Waterlooville. When I wrote the post on Wednesday evening I honestly thought Swansea City would be too strong for the non League side and this was a game too far. They proved me wrong. Fantastic!

I believe that Havant & Waterlooville's progress to the next round means that this is the first time that a team from the sixth level of the English game has reached the Fourth Round Proper since Woking in 1991. We have had to wait seventeen years for this.

The planning down in Hampshire has already started, and questions are already being asked about the amount of travelling support that 'The Hawks' will take up to Merseyside. The FA have already offered the Havant & Waterlooville team the use of the England coach; one assumes Brian Barwick was referring to the bus rather than Fabio Capello.

The amount of support than non League clubs get for the bigger Cup games has, as long as I care to remember, been a topic that stirs strong feelings in some quarters. It is something I have come across many times, and has also surfaced several times in my FA Cup exploits this season. It annoys me somewhat.

I've lost count of the number of times I have heard or read complaints

The Dream Had Become Reality

about the larger attendances that the small clubs suddenly get when a bigger team comes into town. The phrase "glory hunters" is often banded around in reference to the additional floating support that swells the gates. If I had one pound for every time I have heard someone moaning at a Cup game that "most of these fans won't be here next week" or "all these glory hunters come out of the woodwork now, don't they", I'd be a reasonably rich man.

It happened at the Staines Town v Stockport County game that I attended in the First Round this season, back in November. On what was a fantastic evening for Staines, with a League club scalped and a ground full to bursting, there was one grouchy old soak stood in front of me who was complaining about the size of the crowd and that all these "extras" who are not the hard core Staines support should stay away. Really. I had to bite my lip.

A very small part of me sympathises. 179 fans one week for a match against North Greenford United and then just under 2,900 turn up to watch Stockport County. The regulars, who watch the team week in, week out, are bound to wonder where the additional two thousand plus fans come from. It is only natural. But if you follow through their argument, are these people really suggesting that the floating fans stay away from the big games? Do they really want an empty ground for what is such a special, rare event? No matter how much I think on this, I simply cannot fathom the argument.

Surely, this is what it is all about. The swollen gates, the first time visitors and the fans from other clubs in the area. This is a key ingredient that has made the FA Cup one of the best football competitions in the world. How often can a smaller team such as Staines Town, Chasetown, Horsham or Havant & Waterlooville get the opportunity to meet (and beat) League opposition? It comes around infrequently for the majority of non League clubs. For some, never. It is exactly the rarity of such occasions that makes them so appealing when they do occur.

The Dream Had Become Reality

It is something different, unique, out of the ordinary, special, exciting. It is a change from the norm. It is something that just does not happen every day. A good Cup run raises the profile of a club, locals get interested, the town wakes up and takes notice. True, many will only ever come to these attractive games. The vast majority won't be rearranging their Saturday plans to return for a League game against Chelmsford City the following week. But a few might. Or if not then, perhaps later in the season.

If the grounds of non League clubs were not filled to the rafters for these big Cup games, it would be even more surprising. Imagine the scenario. Staines Town v Stockport. Only regulars allowed in. Attendance 170. No TV cameras. No local interest. No floating support. And therefore, no different from North Greenford United. Just another game. Nothing out of the ordinary, nothing to get excited about. No cracking Cup atmosphere. The season, and all future seasons, would become rather boring and rather tame. It simply would not happen.

There is a distinct lack of interest in the Watford v Wolves tie that I will be going to, simply because these clubs play in the same League and actually meet the week after the Cup game. It is nothing special for many supporters and it has not fired the imagination of either set of fans. Now, if either were playing Liverpool - different story.

A natural instinct for us humans is to crave change, to look for something different, something that will appeal, something out of the ordinary, something that raises our excitement levels. If we didn't have this, if we lived life on a constant, unchanging level, with no peaks and highs, what kind of life would that be?

Without the lows, one cannot appreciate the highs. And every now and then along comes an FA Cup fixture that jumps out and screams at you: *"Hey, this is great, this is an exception, how often do you see something like this? Once in a lifetime, if you're lucky! Bloody hell, give me some of that!"*

The Dream Had Become Reality

The Staines Town v Stockport fixture did exactly this for many people, including me. So did Horsham v Swansea City. And Chasetown v Port Vale. Liverpool v Havant & Waterlooville certainly will. Try telling Havant & Waterlooville that they should only take regular supporters (a few hundred?) to Anfield, and no more. What a load of tosh.

Six thousand Luton Town fans travelled to Liverpool for their replay on Wednesday, and they were a credit to the club. Despite losing 5-0 they sang their hearts out for ninety minutes and thoroughly enjoyed what was a massive occasion. It is something special that will live with those that made that trip (on a horribly wet and windy Wednesday) for a long, long time. Imagine what it would have been like if they had got a result.

So to those of you who moan about the floating support, I'm sorry, I just don't get it.

Now, please excuse me, I must go; I have to give an interview for 'The Birmingham Mail'. Now that is something that doesn't happen every day.

The Times They Are a-Changin'

I have got tickets for the game. I contacted Watford FC at the beginning of the week and spoke to a very helpful lady in the ticket office and I was able to buy over the phone. What's more, they arrived this evening. So it's all systems go for Saturday.

I must thank all the Watford and Wolves fans who have kindly contacted me with offers of help to get me a ticket should I fail by the usual means. This from complete strangers. I must also thank the Wolves press officer (Paul) who also offered to help. I am genuinely grateful for everyone's support; you all know who you are.

So, I have the tickets. I am now on the 'database' at Watford FC. I am now the proud owner of fan identification number. I was able to pay over the phone with a (well used) piece of plastic.

This is all a far cry from how it used to be when I was lad growing up watching football. To turn up at the turnstile with a 50p coin was usually all it took. Sometimes a jump over a poorly maintained fence would do the trick. Nowadays it isn't quite so simple. Fan ID numbers, membership schemes, automatic turnstiles, hologram embossed and security coded tickets. All-seater stadiums. Carefully controlled access into and inside grounds. Health & Safety. No smoking. No drinks in the stands. £5 for a prawn sandwich.

Times certainly are a changing. In fact, times have already changed.

This puts me in mind of a story I read a couple of weeks ago. It relates to a different sport (cricket) but the message is still the same.

The story was about a retired clergyman who goes by the name of Dennis Hibbert. Mr. Hibbert was a very keen cricketer and he was an

The Times They Are a-Changin'

active member of his local cricket club near Nottingham. Mr. Hibbert has, in early January of this year, had a ban lifted, a ban that saw him excluded from going onto the premises of his cricket club. The thing is, this ban was handed to Mr. Hibbert seventy years ago. Seventy years of exclusion. It must have been something pretty serious, way back in 1938, which led to an almost life-time ban? His crime? He called a fellow player "a big fat fool".

In this day and age, if a participant in any sport - cricket, rugby and least of all football - questioned a fellow player's body size or mental acumen in such a turn of phrase, barely an eyelid would be batted.

Times certainly have changed, and watch any football game nowadays and it is plain for all to see. Long gone are the halcyon days of players respecting players, fans respecting fans, referees getting the respect they deserve. When did it all start to change? When did that respect disappear from the game? When did players start to verbally abuse referees, fans start to fight? This erosion of respect started at some point in our history. It then grew into disrespect which, way down the line, manifested itself into hooliganism. Years of festering disrespect somehow evolved into street battles between opposing supporters. Football grounds became grounds of war. Train stations and motorway services became no-go zones. Hooligan firms were formed. And then Heysel happened. This tragic event was swiftly followed by the (non-hooligan related) Bradford City fire and the awful scenes that unfolded at Hillsborough.

And out of those dark years the Government had no choice but to take radical action. And this is where we find ourselves today. All-seater stadiums. Membership schemes. Controlled segregation. And databases with fan identification numbers.

Maybe it all started to change when Mr. Hibbert called his team mate a "big fat fool"? But that is an awfully heavy burden to lay on one man's shoulders, and totally unjustified. So I won't even go there.

Now, where did I put those tickets...?

Laugh? I Nearly Started

My wife makes me laugh, so much at times it makes me cry.

Between mid September and mid October last year I saw Dartford play five times in the FA Cup. And in the days prior to every one of those matches my wife would ask where am I going next. "Is it Watford?" she would enquire. And each time I would need to remind her that it is Dartford, not Watford. I would hear her on the phone to family or friends: "yeah, he's off to Watford again this weekend". No matter how many times I corrected her, she still mixed the two places up. They say that men don't listen. It became a bit of a joke.

Then, lo and behold, fate sends me off to Watford for tomorrow's Fourth Round match. You can see where this is going, can't you? At the beginning of the week she asked me whether I had got "the Dartford tickets yet?" On Wednesday my brother-in-law came over to watch the Arsenal game; to complicate matters he explained that he is working in Dartford this week, at which point my wife pipes up "that's where Wolves are playing on Saturday". Even my son joined in "can I come to Dartford with you on Saturday?" I've given up now, there's no point. The icing on the cake was when my brother-in-law left after the Arsenal drubbing; my wife shouted after him "hope the work in Watford goes OK".

Good grief!

Anyway, tomorrow's game. I'm looking forward to it, I think it will be a close affair. The bookies can't separate the two teams and this is the only tie that ensures a Championship team will reach the next round. I have mentioned in previous posts that there has been a smattering of ambivalence amongst the Watford and Wolves fans about the game. I was a perhaps somewhat harsh; I have since been contacted by a

Laugh? I Nearly Started

number of fans from both clubs who are looking forward to the game simply because it is an FA Cup game. The FA Cup still holds its old magic to some supporters; we are now getting into the business end of the competition and there are only four ties to negotiate before a trip to Wembley beckons.

To go and watch your team play at Wembley is still a dream for many fans. I heard the utter disappointment in the Everton fan's voices after they lost midweek to Chelsea, one step away from a trip down the M6 and the M1 to the new national stadium. Many Everton fans felt confident of disposing of Chelsea in the Semi-Final of the Carling Cup, and some of those fans described the defeat as "heartbreaking".

Look at how the Tottenham fans reacted to their mauling of Arsenal. The place was rocking, my TV almost fell off it's stand. Admittedly, a victory over Arsenal, for the first time since 1999, would send any Spurs fan berserk; but I know that the thought of day out at Wembley in February played a part in the celebrations of both the Spurs fans and the Spurs players.

In the FA Cup tonight, tomorrow and on Sunday, players and fans will start to dream of a Wembley appearance. Maybe not so much to some of the smaller teams still in the competition - Havant & Waterlooville have reached their 'Wembley' already and I'm thrilled for the club - but certainly for clubs like Watford and Wolves, with a good wind and a kind draw, the prospect of a Wembley visit may start to become more conceivable.

There are some great games to watch out for this weekend. The match at Anfield is the pick of the bunch for me (and surprise, surprise, it is not being televised). But other games are equally intriguing. Peterborough United host West Bromwich Albion in what should be a good game, with both teams banging in the goals this season. A possible shock on the cards there? Barnet v Bristol Rovers also appeals with both teams beating higher placed opposition in replays this week. That tie guarantees

Laugh? I Nearly Started

a team outside of the top two Leagues in the Fifth Round Proper. Other attractive games include Mansfield against Middlesborough and the battle of the roses between Oldham Athletic and Huddersfield Town. Even Arsenal against Newcastle offers plenty for two teams that have been in the news so much recently.

If you are off to an FA Cup game this weekend, I hope you get to see some entertaining football.

And finally, back to something else that made me laugh this week. Another cracking looking fixture tomorrow is the FA Cup tie between Portsmouth and Plymouth Argyle, two teams with an abundance of passionate support. On the radio this morning I heard that Harry Redknapp, Portsmouth manager, has offered an unusual incentive to Benjani Mwaruwari, the Pompey striker. If he scores a hat-trick in tomorrow's game, Harry Redkanpp will provide Benjani with Fish & Chips for the rest of the season.

I think I'll have Fish & Chips tonight; that will set me up nicely for my trip to Dartford. Sorry, Watford.

Watford 1 Wolverhampton Wanderers 4
Fourth Round Proper Saturday 26 January 2008
Attendance 12,719
Distance travelled 58 miles

I have been watching some of the Africa Cup of Nations in the last few days. There have been entertaining games, plenty of goals and colourful crowds. In fact, some very colourful crowds. The fans at this tournament, and in all previous tournaments, are extolled for their vivid, vibrant attire - a kaleidoscopic of lush colour. Each game I have seen has had one thing in common; the passion of the supporters. The non-stop singing and chanting, and the sheer exuberance in the way each goal is celebrated. Each goal, each corner, each free kick. But it is more than that; it is the constant noise from both sets of supporters irrespective of the performance of the team on the pitch. Unconditional support. It has been a breath of fresh air to watch.

Driving the short distance up the M25 to Watford, I was thinking about the colour that would be on show for this Fourth Round encounter. The yellow, black and red of Watford and the black and gold of Wolves. And that turned out to be the case. The interior of Vicarage Road, as one would expect, is all yellow and red. It was another 'kids for a quid' day and the children were decked out in their colourful Watford replica shirts and scarves, some donned brightly coloured wigs. The Wolves fans added their own club colours to the canvas. Even the players joined in with an array of coloured football boots; blues, oranges and reds. On a bright sunny day the contrasts seemed all the more intense.

Lots of colour. But no passion. From the home fans at any rate. I can't recall going to a ground where the home support has been so muted. The Wolves fans were in a buoyant, party mood and more of that later, but the support from the Hertfordshire faithful was rather hushed. Maybe this was justified. If I'm honest, I was surprised by this result. To be brutally honest, Wolves thoroughly deserved it and Watford's performance was disappointingly poor. In this context, one could excuse the reticence of the home support. The attendance (12,719) was low by Watford's standard; this didn't help matters.

Game 12 Watford 1 Wolverhampton Wanderers 4

Both teams ran out to the theme tune of the 'Z-Cars' - Everton were the first club to use this (mid-sixties) but other clubs, including Watford, adopted the tune. It wasn't long after the start that a bit of smash and grab occurred. Wolves took the lead on five minutes when Andy Keogh calmly chipped Richard Lee in the Watford goal. Some Watford fans were still making their way to the seats but the Wolves following, approximately 2,000, were celebrating wildly and keeping the stewards, between them and the pitch, well occupied.

Watford's first real chance came after ten minutes when Jobi McAnuff shot wide from range, but the Wolves game plan became evident early on. Happy to sit back and soak up Watford pressure, they relied on Keogh and Boothroyd getting behind the Watford back line with Matt Jarvis supporting quickly from midfield whenever they won the ball.

Watford were unfortunate not to equalise after fifteen minutes when a well taken free kick from the edge of the area by Ellington cannoned off the post with the Wolves goalkeeper well beaten. This turned out to be a pivotal point in the game; an equaliser for Watford there may have changed the course of events. The remainder of the first half saw equal possession from both sides and a number of corners from both teams; control of the game see-sawed from one team to another. In this period, the Watford boss Aidy Boothroyd was patently not happy and he could be seen berating his side after several chances had fallen to Wolves, one of which forced a good save out of Richard Lee.

The Watford fans had little to cheer. The biggest excitement in our section of the stand was the news coming through from Anfield of Havant & Waterlooville taking an early lead and then leading for a second time against Liverpool. Magnificent. The half-time whistle went and the teams departed to the Wolves cheers and Watford jeers.

Watford were caught napping at the back when, within minutes of the restart, Keogh was put through into acres of space but, with only the goalie to beat, his effort was tame.

Game 12 Watford 1 Wolverhampton Wanderers 4

This sparked an injection of urgency from Watford, who were also spurred on after a likely earful from Boothroyd in the dressing room and the home team started to turn the screw; first a shot from the angle into the side netting and then a couple of corners in quick succession. The Watford fans responded to this and the noise levels increased; Watford continued to press. But one could sense that the next goal would go a long way to determining the outcome of the match.

Slightly against the run of play, it went to the away team on fifty eight minutes when Elliott was set up by Keogh after good work from Jarvis. The Wolves support once again erupted and the afternoon's first rendition of "Wembeeerleeey, Wembeeerleeey..." filled the ground. Ten minutes later, the game was effectively over. Keogh and Jarvis combined well once again and this time Boothroyd applied the finish. 3-0 to Wolves and cue a big exodus from the home fans and more manic scenes in the Wolves end.

Many of those that left would have missed an almost immediate response when, after a scramble in the penalty area, John-Joe O'Toole (what a great name!) stabbed in from close range. Watford refused to lie down and managed another spell of pressure but failed to make it count. The final nail in Watford's coffin arrived on full-time with a crisp strike from Keogh. I might have been hearing things, but I could have sworn that there were chants of "there's only one Mick McCarthy" from the Wolves faithful.

I enjoyed the game and despite the scoreline it was quite an end to end encounter. The big difference was that Wolves found more space on the break and the Wolves' players seemed to have an edge over Watford's; they looked sharper and quicker in the key areas and made the most of the counter attack. For me, Andy Keogh was man of the match but he was pushed close by Matt Jarvis. Wolverhampton Wanderers march convincingly into the Fifth Round and will (like me) eagerly await Monday's draw.

Game 12 Watford 1 Wolverhampton Wanderers 4

I was joined on this trip once again by Cup stalwarts PB, Mackem, and Captain Beaky who was suffering with a heady mix of night-before Guinness and pre-match Balti pies (plural). He wasn't the only one to suffer the effects and we were all thankful for only a short car journey home.

Reports on the way back mentioned that Mick McCarthy had his Sat Nav stolen from his car. If his players continue to perform like this in the FA Cup, he might well need a replacement for directions to Wembley.

As for Watford, they were distinctly off colour.

Draw for the Fifth Round Proper: Cardiff City v Wolverhampton Wanderers.

For the first time since 1957, all sixteen ties in the Fourth Round were resolved at the first attempt, no replays. Of the sixteen clubs left in the competition, there are only two that I have never visited before. One is Middlesbrough... the other is Cardiff City.

So off across the bridge and through the £5.30 toll, a trip I am extremely familiar with as my sister lives in Carmarthen, South Wales. I'll be able to set the car to auto-pilot and then just remember to exit the M4 at Cardiff.

Croeso i Cymru.

Déjà Vu

I've kind of had a feeling, a premonition if you like, that I would end up going to Cardiff City. Don't ask me why, but the thought has been ricocheting around my vacuous skull ever since I started this journey back in August.

This may well be a trick of the imagination, a sleight of the mind. A bit like déjà vu, when you get that unerring sense that you have done this before, or have had that exact same conversation before. That strong sensation of familiarity. The brain is a complex thing. Of course I may well have thought about the prospect of visiting every single League club at some point in the last six months. Maybe I would be writing this no matter which team had come out of the plastic bowl on Monday. But for some reason, I get that feeling now that Cardiff City was bound to happen. It's all a bit spooky really.

So I wasn't at all surprised with the draw, you could say I expected it. It is a good one for me because I have never been to a game at Ninian Park, home of the Bluebirds. Another ground to tick off the (imaginary) list that I have hidden in some dark recess of of my subconscious.

After the initial adrenalin rush that normally follows a draw for the next round, when the 'things I now need to do' part of my brain goes into meltdown, the fog is now beginning to clear. The journey should be easy enough; only a couple of hours off down the M4. Finding the ground should not pose any problems either as directions appear straight forward.

As for the getting my hands on tickets, I'm in a positive frame of mind thanks to valuable advice already proffered by some very helpful Cardiff fans. First indications are that this game may not be a sell out. Once again, the game will be effectively 'all-ticket' for the away fans. Wolves

Déjà Vu

operate a loyalty points scheme so making that particular route to a ticket a non-starter for me. It is unlikely to be 'all-ticket' for home fans. Even if it was, I should be able to buy tickets through the Cardiff City ticket office as the likelihood of a mass stampede to the ticket office window is slim. A couple of Cardiff supporters have stepped up to the plate to offer their help with tickets should my own efforts go pear shaped; more selfless generosity from people I don't know, only a matter of days after the draw.

The televised games were announced today and, shock of all shocks, three of the four ties selected for television involve a Premiership team. No surprise that the BBC plumped for the big one involving Manchester United and Arsenal. Cardiff City and Wolves have been politely ignored, like a bad smell in a lift. Talking of TV coverage, I noticed this statement from the BBC website that made me smile. This wording appeared at the top of the page listing the eight Fifth Round games, before any of the television coverage had been decided:

"Please note: Fixtures are subject to change. The BBC is not responsible for any changes that may be made".

Er, sorry? Are not the BBC, once they have pointed their collective broadcasting finger at an FA Cup fixture, responsible for that fixture consequently changing? I wonder if the BBC are oblivious to the irony in that statement? Probably.

Back to our game, Cardiff City v Wolverhampton Wanderers, to be played on Saturday 16th February. It will be game number thirteen for me. It has not been chosen to be beamed into millions of homes around the world. Another all-Championship Cup tie that will be spared the limelight that the cameras bring but instead will be served up in the flesh only to a select few thousand who choose to push turnstile.

I've a strange feeling that has happened before on this FA Cup run. A case of déjà vu?

Bubble, Bubble, Toil And Trouble

The kick-off time for the Cardiff City v Wolves game in the Fifth Round of the FA Cup has still not been set. All the other non-televised FA Cup ties on Saturday 16th February will kick-off at 3pm. There is a belief, in some quarters, that the police will have a say in the start time; a 1pm kick-off is expected, although not yet confirmed by Cardiff City FC.

I'm pretty confident that the police will have their say as the potential for crowd trouble at this game is high, due to it being a magnet for the 'hooligan element'. It saddens me to feel obliged to mention the subject in this blog, but it is an issue that I have been unable to ignore since the draw was made.

There is a history of crowd trouble between rival fans, but also a history of disagreement between the two clubs of how best to tackle the problem. Fighting between 'supporters' at games between the two clubs over the years, has not been uncommon, but events off the pitch came to a head in January last year when Wolves banned Cardiff City fans from attending a League game at Molineux. Cardiff City fans felt aggrieved at that decision. There has been a call from some quarters that the Wolves fans should be banned from this Cup game at Cardiff, but I don't believe FA rules will allow that.

There is also debate about the amount of tickets Wolves fans will be allocated for the game. FA Cup rules state that away teams must be offered 15% of the ground capacity, which would mean that Wolves will be offered 3,000 tickets. If Wolves decide to accept this amount, there are big questions about which part of Ninian Park will be used to safely house the away contingent. There are concerns that the end that traditionally houses the home fans will be used for the away support instead, which may in turn reduce the ground's capacity.

Bubble, Bubble, Toil And Trouble

But there is more. There is a belief that this will be a 'bubble' game. This is the bit that saddens me most. A bubble game is effectively a police measure to control away travelling support and comes in many guises. But the principles are always the same. A common example of a bubble game is this: away fans are only allowed to travel on designated club coaches. These coaches are met some distance away from the ground by police, normally at a motorway service station. Here, the police hand out tickets for the match in exchange for pre-paid vouchers. The coaches are then escorted straight to the away fans turnstiles at the ground. After the game, the away fans stay in the ground for a lengthy period (half an hour to an hour or even longer) and then are marched in a heavy police cordon back to the coaches. The coaches are then given a police escort out of the vicinity.

A huge police operation, no freedom for the fans, no independent travel allowed. Watching football in a police bubble.

I have attended games in a bubble before. It is not nice. A regularly used police control measure from the 1970s and 1980s, I was quite shocked to discover that this still happens nowadays at football matches in England and Wales. It seems to happen often to Cardiff City fans, who have become almost accustomed to bubble games on journeys outside of Wales.

So this, our FA Cup game in a couple of week's time, could be a bubble game for Wolves fans. A far cry from the mixed terraces of Dartford, Bromley and Eastbourne Borough. Very sad. Is this what some football fans still have to endure simply to watch ninety minutes of football? Is it really worth it?

But there is a more important question. This is a situation that the hooligan minority, still present at many clubs, are responsible for creating. Is this something that they are proud of?

Do they really care? I'm afraid that the answer is probably "no".

Home In Hong Kong

Tomorrow, on Saturday 9th February, Chertsey Town will entertain Bedfont Green in a Combined Counties Football League game. Camberley Town travel to Raynes Park Vale. For Dartford it's a trip to AFC Sudbury whilst Eastbourne Borough welcome Dorchester Town.

Not particularly newsworthy, you might think. Important games for those non League clubs, teams that I have enjoyed watching on this FA Cup run. But on a day when the big football news is a million miles away from the non League scene, I felt those fixtures were worthy of mention. Hold that thought.

Meanwhile, the unavoidable football news in all the papers today is the talk of proposals for Premier League games to be played in various cities around the world. The globalisation of football. The story is on the back page of every major paper, and even on the front page of some.

I really can't quite grasp the enormity of what I have been reading. The story first broke yesterday with a statement from the Premier League that they are to investigate the possibility of certain English games being played in venues in America, Asia, Africa and Oceania with major cities bidding for the right to host games. What's more, the matches will be played out between top flight clubs, they will be additional League fixtures - an extra ten games - and League points will be up for grabs. Billed as an 'international round', these will played in January each year and fixtures will be drawn at random. So Arsenal may have to play Manchester United in three League matches in one season, whilst Chelsea get to play Derby County three times.

The reaction has been strong (to say the least) and the idea is already being denounced by players, managers, fans and press alike. At the root of the proposals, not unsurprisingly, is money. The opportunity for the

Home In Hong Kong

Premier League (not the FA) to capitalise on the phenomenal marketability of our beloved game around the world. It has been coming for some time; more and more foreign owners have invested in our game; club tours to America and Asia have become the norm; merchandise sales in countries such as Korea and Japan far outweigh sales in England. The Premier League want to be in on the TV rights that will come with this globalisation deal, something that will be worth millions.

Money talks.

I heard Gareth Southgate this morning say "this will not happen". Harry Redknapp said "it will happen eventually, it has been coming for some time". I heard West Ham fans explain that, once again, the real supporters are being priced out of the game. That "the clubs don't care about the fans". Understandable views.

That is not all. Will clubs really want to drag their players halfway around the world in January? Will the National Game - the FA - support an idea that is going to add to the number of games that players will play in a single season at a time when there is a call for a reduction in the number of games?

My own view? Well, that has lurched from utter disbelief, through mild shock and on to thinking of the implications of this idea; and therefore implied acceptance that yes, this could actually happen. In football terms, this is massive news, and it will stay on the back pages for a long, long time. You will read and listen to the whole gambit of reaction to it over the next few weeks and probably longer. Who can say whether it really will come to fruition or not? Certainly not me. But for what it is worth, I can't think of a single good reason for doing this.

But if it does happen it will, in my humble opinion, be a sad day for football in our country. Football will become divorced from our heritage. The history will be severed from the very heart of the game. It is this close relationship between present and past, the team of today and the club of yesteryear, that I have seen to be so important for clubs and fans in the course of doing this FA Cup road to Wembley. It means so much to clubs, that sense of heritage which brings with it a sense of belonging for supporters.

But it is more than that; it is the sense of place that is paramount in the game. Fans always go back to their club; a physical location, the ground, that piece of turf in their neighbourhood. Owners come and go. Players come and go. Even some fans do. But the one thing that remains the same, with the exception of the occasionally rare ground move, is the location. The village, the town, the city. The sense of place is what matters.

If football really does go global, what will happen? Many years down the line, will we end up with a closed League of four, six or eight clubs that will only ever play on foreign soils? Will we no longer see the top four teams play in our own country? Watching Arsenal play in Beijing will, for the majority, be as practically impossible as it is for most of us to watch Barcelona, Real Madrid or Boca Juniors. Being able to afford the match ticket for a game in North London is difficult for many as it is. The elite teams will disappear out of range; out of pocket and, quite possibly, out of mind.

Who knows? Maybe a new 'top four' will grow in the place vacated by the globetrotters. Like a new shoot growing from a scythed tree, new names will emerge to fill the void. Located still within our shores, the likes of Everton, Aston Villa, Tottenham and Blackburn will become the big English clubs. For many, Arsenal, Manchester United, Liverpool and Chelsea, with their new bases in Tokyo, Melbourne, Johannesburg and Los Angeles will become distanced both physically and financially. They will be playing with themselves.

There is some precedent, albeit on a smaller scale. It has already happened with Wimbledon; uprooted and carted off to Milton Keynes, the loss of that sense of place was just too much for many fans to bear

Home In Hong Kong

and AFC Wimbledon was born out of the withered stump of the old club. And in protest of the foreign ownership buying into the brand that is Manchester United, FC United came into being.

So whilst you are reading all about these plans for globalisation of our game, and the expert judgements that will inevitably come to pass, bear in mind it will only affect the top few clubs in our game. The elite. Meanwhile, the real football continues. The games at Chertsey Town, Camberley Town, Dartford and Eastbourne Borough will still be played out. The smaller clubs will still strive for greater things; they will still have their FA Cup dreams and yearn for their moments in the spotlight. They will still want to push on up through the football pyramid and on to greater things.

But how far will they now want to go. To League football? Undoubtedly. To the Premier League? Probably, yes.

But to Beijing? Or to a home in Hong Kong?

You tell me.

Incognito

A rather strange thing happened to me this evening. I popped into the local '24-7' store, the one that is not actually open 24 hours a day, nor 7 days week. I bought two pints of milk (green), one last minute Valentine's card (no expense spared, don't tell my wife), and a copy of the Surrey Herald (Chertsey, Addlestone, Byfleet and Woking edition). I don't always buy the Surrey Herald, but there, on the front page, was yours truly. I knew I would be in today's edition, so was not surprised. Alongside my mug shot (that same mug that is best suited for radio) was the headline:

"Fan-tastic! What starts in Chertsey and ends at Wembley Stadium? Find out on page 5".

Would that make you want to turn to page 5?

But the strange thing that happened in the shop was that the young Bulgarian girl (or is she Polish?) behind the counter smiled and pointed in the general direction of my picture on the front page of the newspaper, then smiled again before she whipped a £20 note from my fingers. At least I think she did, it all happened so quickly.

Good grief! Have I been recognised? In this sleepy Surrey backwater, someone in my local shop associated me with the newspaper article? No, surely not. When I started this blog, I deliberately wanted to keep my identity hidden, mainly because I realise how sad and inane all of this is.

My real name is not 'Sniffer 72' (my blog pseudonym); I know my parents have a warped sense of humour, but not that much. I am not really 93. I do not have a photo of me on this site.

Incognito

I have had my ramblings appear in a couple of magazines, and in a number of football programmes. But no photos of me. My picture did appear on the back page of the Birmingham Mail two weeks ago but as I rarely visit Birmingham that blip in the revelation of my identity would hardly register. The South Wales Echo is due to call; if they do a piece I will send in a picture of someone else. Some 'friends' would suggest Bruce Forsyth.

There are a number of reasons people choose to go incognito. But this weekend, at Cardiff, the Wolves fans are going to stick out like sore thumbs. For reasons of safety and for reasons of policing, this game at Cardiff will, as I have previously mentioned, be a bubble game for the Wolves supporters. They will travel from Wolverhampton on designated coaches. They will be met away from the ground by the police who will hand out tickets. They will be escorted down the motorway (all exits blocked) and rushed through Cardiff, ignoring all the red lights as they are waved through. They will be paraded to the ground in an envelope of blue flashing lights which will announce "We're Here!" Their arrival at the ground will be heralded by barking police dogs and on-edge policemen and policewomen barking instructions.

I have been made aware of the dilemma that a number of Wolves fans face. Not allowed to travel independently, those who do not live in Wolverhampton have a tough decision to make. Is it worth travelling up to Wolverhampton to then travel by coach to Cardiff? For two Wolves fans in particular, one who actually lives in Cardiff, another in Bristol, the answer is "no", it is not worth it. And that is a shame.

Some Wolves fans will have bought tickets through Cardiff, probably online to conceal their identity. So some Wolves fans will be sitting or standing in amongst the Cardiff fans. Is this what the South Wales Police had in mind when these travelling restrictions were set? Is this going to make it safe for all concerned? Those few Wolves fans in the home ends may choose to remain incognito.

Incognito

One thing is for sure. I'll remain unrecognised in Cardiff despite the fact that I may have been spied in a local shop in Chertsey. Did I really get recognised in the shop? Perhaps not, I probably just imagined it. Then when I got back from the '24-7' - just before it closed - I realised my friend behind the counter had short-changed me.

Now *that's* why she was smiling.

Cardiff City 2 Wolverhampton Wanderers 0
Fifth Round Proper Saturday 16 February 2008
Attendance 15,339
Distance travelled 308 miles

Two quick-fire goals in the first eleven minutes of this game settled the tie for the team from Wales against a very poor Wolves side. Any club that belts out Stone Roses in the build up to kick-off gets my nod of approval; with the appropriate 'This Is The One' still hanging on the cold Cardiff air as the game started, one could sense from the home team and home support that this was indeed the one they had waited for.

On a gloriously bright day, Cardiff effectively killed off the Wolves bright and early, and the men from the Midlands failed to recover.

My day had started a little frantically. I once again travelled with my good mates PB and Mackem (and to later meet Captain Beaky and Posh Mate at the ground, the latter returning to the FA Cup fray after a short absence). I went on air on talkSPORT radio just before departure for the 150 mile trip to South Wales. I don't know how many of you heard my five minutes of fame, and I haven't heard the piece yet myself, but I think I failed in my shameless attempt to lay claim to Mike Parry's FA Cup Final ticket. I don't think he was too impressed.

The journey down to Cardiff went without hitch. I even managed to lob the £5.30 in loose change into the coin bin at the Severn Bridge without embarrassingly missing. I wonder how many drivers have failed to hit the target and realised that, rolling off down towards the Severn with their last pound coin, was their only chance of getting into Wales? Probably quite funny to watch as well. They should erect spectator galleries.

The ground itself was easy to find and parking was quite straightforward. There is an awful lot of construction work south and west of Ninian Park; this is where the old Cardiff Athletics Stadium is making way for the new Cardiff ground and work is well underway. As you drop down off the M4 at junction 33 and drive towards the ground on Leckwith Road you get a great view of Ninian Park with the Millennium Stadium

Game 13 Cardiff City 2 Wolverhampton Wanderers 0

as a backdrop. The old and the new.

Without being too critical of Ninian Park, it has an old feel to it, which isn't a bad thing. We sat in the Grandstand which sits astride one length of the pitch, with the Spar Family Stand to the left ("So near, so Spar") and the Bob Bank opposite. Our seats were of the dated wooden variety and the place had a whiff of olden days feel to it. This is what gives Ninian Park its character.

That and the great atmosphere generated by the passionate home fans. It is no exaggeration to say that this was the noisiest game I have been to on this Cup run, the atmospheres at Wolves and Watford in previous rounds were tame in comparison. The home fans were vocal from all four sides of the pitch and the great start to the game resulted in the old Ninian Park roof being almost lifted from the stands. The Wolves fans, before the game started, also played their part in raising the volume level.

Wolves were poor. Mick McCarthy summed up his team's display with a single word. "Hopeless". Wolves arrived in South Wales with four Cup-tied players, their influential Michael Kightly injured and another key player, Darren Ward, awaiting the arrival of his child. Michael Gray, who had played so poorly in the Third Round game with Cambridge United and was absent in the marvellous Wolves performance at Watford, was back in the team. A coincidence that Wolves played poorly yet again with Gray in the team? Perhaps. The whole of the Wolves rearguard failed to play well, with Gary Breen looking especially out of his depth.

As for Cardiff, they started like a runaway train and simply could not be caught. The first goal came after only two minutes. Jimmy Floyd Hasselbaink slid the ball through a wandering Wolves defence into the path of Peter Whittingham. As Hasselbaink made the pass he was taken out with a late challenge; all credit to referee Rob Styles who played the advantage when many would have blown up. Whittingham had acres of time and space to calmly slot home beyond the advancing Wayne

Game 13 Cardiff City 2 Wolverhampton Wanderers 0

Hennessey. The place erupted. 1-0 to Cardiff City.

The old ground was positively rocking after eleven minutes. Hasselbaink began and finished off a move that resulted in a goal to grace any game. This was a quality goal, and is certainly a contender for my own goal of this road to Wembley journey. Hasselbaink once again found the ball at his feet in the centre circle. With the Wolves back four all over the place, Hasselbaink was able to pick out Paul Parry on the left wing. The subsequent cross over the back-peddling Wolves defence was a bit too heavy but the ball eventually made its way back to Hasselbaink on the edge of the box. With one shoulder drop and a touch inside his marker, Hasselbaink unleashed a dipping left footed shot into the top corner. Fantastic. To a man, the Cardiff crowd rose to salute a great goal. This really was gripping stuff and Cardiff were on their way.

After that, Wolves struggled to produce anything really meaningful for the remainder of the half even though they did manage to regain some of the possession. The introduction of Freddy Eastwood before the half-time oranges failed to spark Wolves into life. The Wolves supporters' "we want our money back" chants summed up their mood.

In the second half the away team emerged with a little more purpose. Not long after the restart, Kevin Kyle found himself with only the Cardiff stopper Peter Enckelman to beat. Kyle froze and then fluffed and any remaining danger was averted when the Cardiff defender Loovens cleared off the line. With that chance one could sense the life drain from the Wolves team and heads once again went down throughout the side.

Cardiff continued to apply pressure of their own and on two separate occasions Paul Parry had head-to-head contests with the Wolves keeper but on both occasions Hennessey came out on top. The Cardiff midfield then shut up shop for the rest of the game and two excellent performances from Stephen McPhail and Gavin Rae prevented any more opportunities for the away side.

Game 13 Cardiff City 2 Wolverhampton Wanderers 0

The game drifted to the expected conclusion and Cardiff were through, eighty one years after their last appearance in the Quarter-Finals. In a week when the appeal of the FA Cup has once again been questioned, a Cardiff fan seated behind me commented that he would take mid-table obscurity (rather than promotion to the Premier League) in exchange for an FA Cup Final appearance anytime. Believe me, this competition still appeals.

This was a very good game and one that the majority of the 15,339 crowd were happy with. It must have been a long journey back for the travelling support - I wish Wolves well for the rest of the season, I have enjoyed the short Cup run with them. To see Wolves exit the competition without much of a fight was a disappointment for me, but I dare say all those associated with the Black and Gold must be feeling ten times worse.

And so the baton passes to Cardiff City. Based on yesterday's tidy performance Cardiff deserve their place in the next round. As we walked away from the ground engulfed in the cacophony of celebration from the Cardiff fans, I found myself still humming along to the Stone Roses' 'This Is The One'. This is the one the fans had been waiting for.

And boy, I bet it was well worth the wait.

Draw for the Sixth Round Proper: Sheffield United or Middlesbrough v Cardiff City.

Wembley is so close you can almost smell it. Not that the new national stadium gives off an unpleasant odour, but it really is only around the corner. Are we there yet? Actually, not far now. The Quarter-Finals will be held on the weekend of 8th and 9th of March and for all clubs concerned a little matter of two ties away from the Final. The excitement amongst the fans of the remaining clubs is palpable.

Game number fourteen next and a trip up north beckons. I am still to be

Game 13 Cardiff City 2 Wolverhampton Wanderers 0

convinced that I will make it all the way to the Final in May. Although as each day, each game and each round passes, I am enjoying this adventure more and more. In the same way that my mouth starts to water whenever I get a whiff of Marmite, the smell of Wembley is having the same effect.

Wembley Twice?

In the build up to last Saturday's game at Cardiff I was hearing on the grapevine that both the Semi-Finals of this season's FA Cup are to be staged at Wembley. Then confirmation last Sunday (on Match of the Day and on talkSPORT) that indeed, this is to be the case.

I have mixed feelings. On the one hand, it may be a good thing for the practicalities of this FA Cup run. It would, in theory, increase the chances of getting a ticket. The official capacity at the 'Venue of Legends' is 90,000 as opposed to the traditionally used neutral venues of Villa Park (42,640), The Emirates (60,355) and Old Trafford (76,212). There is also no real distance to travel; I would probably leave the car at home for my wife to wash whilst I jump on the train and tube.

On the other hand, assuming that I did actually make it to the Final, having a Semi-Final there would be a bit of an anti-climax. My heart is telling me that Wembley should be reserved for the Final and the Final only. That sense of a special achievement, the grand occasion that is reaching a Final at Wembley, would be diluted somewhat. I could quite perceivably fail in this venture yet still make it to Wembley. That would be a strange feeling indeed.

And what about the fans of the clubs in the last four? A potential Semi-Final tie could be Manchester United v Middlesbrough. Would the fans from either club want to travel down to London in April? More money flowing out of the fans' pockets? Elland Road or Hillsborough would offer 40,000 the chance to see the game, so would it be worth travelling the extra distance for 50,000 extra tickets? Quite possibly.

The decision to hold both games at Wembley was no doubt made some time ago and the bottom line is once again money. The stadium cost an outrageous £778 million to build (compared to the fabulous Allianz

Wembley Twice?

Arena in Munich which came in on budget at £340 million) and it needs to pay for itself. Staging high profile games is the only way it will achieve this.

A not insignificant adjustment to the FA Cup for this season then. An adjustment for the fans as well; it will be amusing to hear the "we're all off to Wembley!" chants in the Semi-Finals. And perhaps a minor adjustment to the title of this blog? - 'Wick to Wembley twice?'

Doesn't quite sound right, does it?

Oh, and if my wife is reading this, then I was joking about her washing my car...

Revised draw for the <u>Sixth Round Proper</u>: Middlesbrough v Cardiff City.

Middlesbrough saw off a determined Sheffield United in their Fifth Round Proper replay. In a game that could have gone either way, fate has intervened once more to send me on my first ever visit to Teesside. Best fill the car up then.

Sons, Fathers And Football

It was all a bit easy in the end. Logged on to the Middlesbrough website around about tea time yesterday (Sunday) and within a few minutes I had bought four tickets for the Cup game against Cardiff City. I have become increasingly pessimistic as each round passes, about my chances of getting tickets; so I was rather chuffed that I got some for next Sunday. Which is why my wife caught me running around the front room with my shirt over my head and my arms outstretched early yesterday evening, à la Ravanelli. Not easy to explain that one away.

The Middlesbrough tickets arrived yesterday. My son asked if one was for him. With the smallest pang of guilt I had to tell him no. He didn't look overly disappointed. He has no concept of the distance we will have to travel on Sunday. Not the best on long car journeys, my eight year old struggles with the eight minute trip to school, so eight hours in the car in a single day would be too much for him. And for me.

My boy loves his football, more so playing than watching. Any father who is into football takes great pride in seeing his child take up the sport. Many, including myself, can't help live their football lives through their child. It is difficult not to.

My son turned eight only recently. For his birthday he asked for a football shirt. A Tottenham Hotspur shirt. Living so close to London it was inevitable that he would end up supporting a London team. As sure as night follows day, he was never going to support my team. A League One team from up north, my team would always be way outside his radar in terms of geographical location and footballing quality.

An eight year old can be easily influenced. My son went through stages of supporting the team of whomever he had seen most recently. If we visited long-time friends from near Warrington, Cheshire, he would declare that he now supported Manchester United. If the son from a friend of the family came for a sleepover, Liverpool would be his team of choice. One of his best friends at school supports Chelsea and my son, for a while, would follow suit. When he attends football courses with Fulham they become flavour of the month. From my own football trips he has grown up wearing a number of different football kits, ranging from England (all the white, red and blue variants) to RC Lens and PSV Eindhoven to Barcelona. My son even supported Dartford for a couple of weeks after I took him down to Princes Park on this FA Cup run back in September. And I plan to take him back. Kids of that age are fickle and understandably so. He is eight and following a number of different teams is not an issue for him.

He used to tell people that he supported every team except my team.

When I myself was a similar age, I remember making a conscious decision about which football team I was going to support. That was a seminal point in my life. I had a choice of supporting my father's team, Manchester City, or a team that my best friend at school supported. I chose the latter. Only now do I realise how much that must have hurt my father. He used to take me to many games at Maine Road, and I hold dear those memories. My father is still a season ticket holder. If I ever said I never once felt slightly guilty about not choosing to support Manchester City, the team the rest of my family support, I would be lying. I harbour a soft spot for them still.

But I am determined not to influence my own son in anyway. He has to choose himself. But when he asked for a Tottenham shirt it arrived like a bolt out of the blue. Of all the London teams he could have gone for, this was the one I had hoped for least. Fulham, Chelsea, Arsenal, Charlton, Crystal Palace - even Reading. But Tottenham? Just like me a generation ago he was influenced by his best mate. His very best friend at school, who he has probably been friends with longest in his short life, supports Tottenham Hotspur and always has. Poor child!

Sons, Fathers And Football

When he asked for the shirt I was shocked. That initial response quickly gave way to a feeling of sickness - that awful stomach churning sensation that comes with the knowledge that you will have to do something you don't really want to do. Something unpleasant, but unavoidable. When I finally went to buy the shirt I asked the teenager behind the counter for a brown paper bag. She looked at me blankly. I couldn't be bothered to explain.

So now my son has another shirt for his collection. I cannot tell him not to wear it. I cannot refuse to take him to a Tottenham game, if he asks. The only saving grace is that if he becomes a true Tottenham supporter, he won't even want to go to watch them. He'll just sit at home and moan. But whatever happens, whatever football choices he makes now or at any point in the future, I will still love him more than I can ever explain.

I just hope this is a phase he's going through and it will pass. I really, really do.

The FA Cup Is Up For Grabs

What a day for the FA Cup! Who would have thought that the remaining two 'top four' Premier League teams, Chelsea and Manchester United, would bow out of the competition today? Fantastic results for Barnsley and Portsmouth who have now both booked a Wembley appearance.

The trip to Middlesbrough is almost upon us - it will be a very early start tomorrow as it will for all the Cardiff fans making the journey. What awaits the fans of Middlesbrough, Cardiff City and those of Bristol Rovers and West Bromwich Albion? Whatever happens, there must be a real sense amongst all fans concerned that the FA Cup is up for grabs. A top four team will not be taking the famous trophy home with them this year.

Another breath of fresh air in what has been an enthralling FA Cup competition this season. Let's just hope I'm there at the end to see the trophy being lifted.

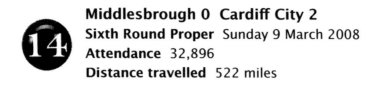

Middlesbrough 0 Cardiff City 2

Sixth Round Proper Sunday 9 March 2008
Attendance 32,896
Distance travelled 522 miles

As I sit down to write this on Monday morning many parts of the country continue to be battered by storms. For two days a maelstrom of sorts tore its way through the FA Cup leaving the form book in tatters. On a special weekend that will live long in the memories of football fans up and down the country and around the world, only one top division side is left standing in the competition. Up at the Riverside on a cold and blustery Sunday, Cardiff City produced a polished display to blow Middlesbrough out of the Cup.

For me, and my fellow travellers - Mackem, PB and Posh Mate - it was a fantastic, tiring and somewhat surreal day. It started huddled against the elements at little after seven o'clock in the morning outside Chertsey Town Football Club. We were to be accompanied on this leg of the FA Cup journey by an ESPN-Star film crew and the day started with a quick interview where it all began back in August. The filming was to continue later in the day (before and after the game) and this added some gloss and sparkle to what was a marvellous occasion.

It was a long journey north but well worth it. We had no problems whatsoever in finding the ground and arrived nice and early. The Riverside sits alone in quite an open spread of a semi-industrial landscape. It dominates the horizon. It is an impressive sight and is by far the biggest ground we have visited on this run. The view from inside the ground, looking back out towards Middlesbrough and its famous transporter bridge straddling the River Tees, is also quite impressive. Parking was easy and getting away after the game (which included us being filmed as we walked off into the sunset) was a doddle.

The game was a sell-out with an official attendance of 32,896; Middlesbrough have been striving for some time to fill the Riverside. There was a real buzz of excitement in and around the ground. Only one game from Wembley, over two hundred and fifty miles away but within

Game 14 Middlesbrough 0 Cardiff City 2

touching distance. Cardiff City had brought with them a considerable following (just under 4,000) and their vocal cords were getting a good run-in well before kick-off. The home support had also been whipped into a frenzy by the stadium announcer. As the teams ran out to 'Papa's Got A Brand New Pigbag' an impressive 6,000 card display in the North Stand (home end) spelt out the words "Sporting Glory". The atmosphere was positively crackling and, even as a neutral, one couldn't help but feel a real part of what was about to unfold.

The crackling evolved into a shock. Another Cup shock.

Middlesbrough simply failed to live up to expectations. In a game where it was difficult to identify the team from the Premier League, Cardiff put in a totally composed and professional performance that left the home team chasing shadows.

As in the Fifth Round game, Cardiff City found themselves nurturing a two goal lead long before half-time. Both teams started brightly and the atmosphere had obviously filtered through to the players. But it was Cardiff who pounced early. A ball was lofted into the Middlesbrough box which appeared to be brought under control by the arm of Stephen McPhail. With the Middlesbrough players appealing and the referee waving play on, Peter Whittingham ignored the protestations; with some extremely neat footwork and a sea of red shirts on top of him, Whittingham somehow dug the ball out from under his feet to send a glorious curling shot beyond Schwarzer and in off the post. A wonderful goal which stunned the home crowd; the away fans in the South Stand exploded with joy which prompted a rather comical 'Keystone Cops' entrance from a number of sprinting policemen across and in front of the Cardiff support to prevent any pitch encroachment. Nine minutes gone and already theatre of high calibre.

If the home crowd were stunned, then so were the home team players. The goal visibly affected the Middlesbrough side. Their game plan seemed to involve hoofing one long ball after another up field. The

Game 14 Middlesbrough 0 Cardiff City 2

intended recipients, Alves or Tuncay, are both gifted players but surely would have benefited with balls played to feet. I had been especially looking forward to seeing Tuncay as he had impressed me this season, but today the game bypassed him. Even the long twenty or thirty yard balls out to Downing on the left were ineffective and Middlesbrough had no outlet on the right as Luke Young frequently balked at stepping over the halfway line.

By contrast, Cardiff were assured and confident in their approach play. They showed better movement both on and off the ball and brought to the match more ideas and invention. The slicker movement heralded a second goal after twenty three minutes. Hasselbaink, who was roundly applauded by all areas of the ground before kick-off, won a free-kick thirty yards out after a clumsy challenge by the gloved Rochemback. From the dead ball, Whittingham curled in a pin point cross to the far post which was met beyond the last defender by a diving Roger Johnson, to send a header back across goal and into the corner. Cardiff in control and the South Stand once again rocking.

Middlesbrough simply had no response. More long balls, more wasted possession and barely capable of stringing more than a couple of passes together. They had only one long range effort from Alves in the first half which was easily parried by Enckelman in the Cardiff goal. Any glimpses of danger from the home team were quickly and ably dealt with by Glenn Loovens and his defensive partners who coped with everything punted towards them. Loovens, for me, was the man of the match.

Middlesbrough had an opportunity at half-time to change their system. But all they did was bring off Alves for Mido and persist in playing the same long ball game that had failed them in the first forty five minutes. The home support were becoming increasingly frustrated and let their feelings be known. Cardiff City were now in complete ascendancy and there was no sign that Middlesbrough were going to break the Welsh team's stranglehold. The second half, although a little scrappy, was still

Game 14 Middlesbrough 0 Cardiff City 2

good to watch. Middlesbrough were utterly disappointing and failed to give Enckelman a single test. Cardiff were content to sit a little deeper, pack the midfield and see out the game. The home fans started to drift out of the stadium with seventy minutes on the clock. For a game that promised so much for the Smoggies, one could sense that they felt totally let down.

Overall, Cardiff City were the only team that looked like winning this tie. The Cardiff fans made the most of the victory and celebrated in style; a cacophony of noise and a swarm of dancing bodies, Welsh flags, giant daffodils and even one bare-chested hardy soul wearing only a pink tutu. I'm sure that their long trip back home would have been one to savour.

Gareth Southgate, in his programme notes, had talked about the need to pass the ball and keep the ball on the floor. I think he forgot to tell his players. There was a huge 'Spirit of Steaua' flag waved in one corner of the game in reference to Middlesbrough's famous UEFA Cup victory over the Romanian team. But this flag was rolled up and packed away long before the final whistle. Middlesbrough can now concentrate on the League whilst Cardiff City are off to Wembley, along with Portsmouth, Barnsley and West Bromwich Albion.

It is one hundred years since an FA Cup Semi-Final line up has included only one top flight team. This season has witnessed an extraordinary and quite remarkable FA Cup competition. We all left Teesside for a long Sunday evening car journey down the M1 sensing that we really had been, and continue to be, involved in something special. Something very, very special. For an FA Cup that people will talk about for years, I and my friends who have joined me already have our own little place in it.

And on a stormy March day, with Wembley in sight, the thought of it simply blows me away.

Draw for the Semi-Final: Barnsley v Cardiff City.

Is This The End Of The Queue?

It is amazing how quickly opinions can change, not least one's own. After Cardiff City's great win at Middlesbrough just over a week ago, I stood in front of the ESPN-Star TV camera outside the Riverside Stadium and said, with an air of confidence, I had a reasonable chance of getting tickets for the Semi-Final at Wembley. I've seen the footage; I even had a wry smile on my face, that kind of smug look that suggested I knew what I was talking about; the look that suggested that I knew something everyone else didn't.

Watching that footage one week on I can re-evaluate the situation. What my expression actually said was "this bloke is talking a load of crap". A week is a long time in football and much has happened since our journey back from Teesside.

First up, as we all know, the draw pitted Cardiff City with Barnsley. Already confident of getting tickets because of the lack of any of the big four in the last four, this draw boosted my confidence even further. The new national stadium has an official capacity of 90,000. In my naivety, I thought that both these Championship teams would get a fair wedge of the allocation. Take off a little for segregation and each team would be looking at around 43,000 tickets. I was already registered on the Cardiff City database and I actually felt quite pleased with myself.

That was on the Monday of last week. Two days later and my mood had changed markedly. Both clubs were having a planning meeting at Wembley on the Thursday to discuss, amongst other things, ticketing arrangements. But by Wednesday news had filtered out that Cardiff City and Barnsley were to get an allocation of only 33,000 tickets each. Confirmation from both clubs followed pretty quickly with additional information that suggested that at least 20,000 tickets were going to Wembley club members and corporate sales. If that is indeed an accurate figure, that is a staggering proportion of the total tickets that fans from neither Cardiff nor Barnsley will be able to get their hands on. Shocking news. My confidence was rapidly seeping from every pore.

The clubs then announced their own ticket sales arrangements. Quite rightly, both clubs are to sell tickets in a phased approach, providing the regular fans with first dibs. At Cardiff, Ambassadors and Season Ticket holders will be able to buy first, followed by Away Travel Members and finally holders of a ticket stub from last week's League game against Hull City. This incentive swelled the gate for Hull's visit to Ninian Park. Good marketing ploy. Additional incentives include extra Semi-Final tickets for Ambassadors or Season Ticket holders who renew for next season if they renew by the end of this week. Barnsley have a similar phased approach for their own ticket sales.

The worrying part for me is that I do not figure in the equation. I do not fall into any of the Cardiff sales categories. I will have to wait for the 'general sale' phase, if there are any tickets left by then. This gave me a glimmer of hope through a door that had been left slightly ajar. But then I heard an announcement from the FA that appeared to slam the door firmly shut in my face. It went something like this:

"The regulations for this game prevent any information regarding general sale being released at this time. The Football Association have stipulated that tickets may only go on general sale should both clubs involved in the fixture have tickets remaining".

This left a massive question. What if one or both clubs had tickets left to sell after their predetermined sales phases had completed? Where do these tickets go? Back to the FA for corporate guests? Back to the clubs for another sales phase? Questions that remain unanswered.

Whilst I was beginning to accept the fact that my chance of getting a ticket for the Semi-Final was virtually non-existent, I was confronted with another, more unexpected emotion. When I started this venture I

Is This The End Of The Queue?

knew it would be a struggle to get tickets in the latter rounds, something I have repeatedly acknowledged. I am even quite surprised I have made it this far; the draw has certainly been very kind to me. But in those early days I envisaged that, if I got this far, I would be competing for a ticket with supporters from the likes of Manchester United, Chelsea, Arsenal or Liverpool. Or any of the other top Premier teams. For some reason, the thought of a fan from one of those clubs missing out on a trip to Wembley, because I had managed to get my sweaty mitts on a ticket instead, didn't really bother me. I felt it was something I could live with.

But now, faced with a scramble for tickets alongside Cardiff and Barnsley fans, it has become something that doesn't really sit comfortably with me. It is an unnerving feeling. Listening to the fans from South Wales and South Yorkshire, it is evident that there will be genuine fans from both sides that will not be able to get tickets. Those who are not Season Ticket holders or Ambassadors or Away Travel members. Those who are exiled in different parts of the country or on foreign soil. Fans that have much more of a right to watch this game. And I find that quite sad. This will be a huge occasion for both clubs. Absolutely massive. An occasion that the bigger clubs and their fans are familiar with. But for these two second tier teams, something quite unique. An FA Cup Semi-Final. An FA Cup Semi-Final at Wembley. Chances are that many fans of either club will not live to see anything like this happen again. What right do I have to a ticket?

Well, that is a much easier question to answer.

So what about that question I was asked in the post-match Teesside chill up at the Riverside last week? If asked again now, I would answer it quite differently. I would not have that smug look on my face. The answer could not be any more different.

But who knows? Ask me again this time next week. A week really is a long time in football.

The Road To Wembley Diamond Car Wobbler

Try telling anyone in Cardiff or Barnsley that the FA Cup doesn't mean anything anymore. The road to Wembley can start anywhere. It can be a long road or it can be short. But actually getting there is a huge achievement, so much more if it is totally unexpected. It is the arriving that means just as much as the journey, don't let anyone tell you otherwise. Cardiff fans and Barnsley fans alike are living the dream.

In Cardiff and in Barnsley the message boards are buzzing. The club websites are failing to play it down, even though they are "taking one game at a time". The local press are loving it. In sharp contrast to Chertsey back in August, Cup fever really has come to town.

With Cup fever comes the Cup merchandise. For example, Cardiff are offering fans the chance to pre-order the FA Cup Semi-Final programme. The £5 programme will cost £11 if you want it delivered to your door. That alone is double my entry fee for the Chertsey Town v Wick game.

The occasion is a money-maker's dream. You must make sure you have all the latest gear before the trip to Wembley. The Road to Wembley Car Window Flag. The Road to Wembley Diamond Car Wobbler. The Foam FA Cup. The Foam Wembley 2008 Hand. The Road to Wembley Mini Car Scarf Wobbler. The Road to Wembley Mini Hand Flag. The FA Cup 2008 Scarf.

And to think I was worried about getting tickets for the big game - I now have other concerns. So I really must dash and order some merchandise for my trip. I'd be mortified if I left it too late to get my hands on a Road to Wembley Diamond Car Wobbler.

Let's wobble all the way to Wembley.

Fever Pitch

FA Cup Semi-Final weekend is here and I am quite excited! Actually, that is a real understatement. I'm not sure if I can contain myself. The tickets for the Sunday game between Cardiff City and Barnsley (as if I needed to tell you who was playing) arrived this morning. They actually arrived yesterday morning but needed a signature so they were lovingly looked after, fed and watered, and tucked up in bed for the night, by the kind custodians down at the Chertsey Post Office. Ready for me to pick up this morning.

More good news yesterday arrived in the form of an announcement that the planned tube strike has been called off. I was cursing when I heard that a strike had been called to start at 6:30pm on Sunday evening, just over half an hour after the end of the game. The thought of over 80,000 fans trying to get away from the new stadium with no tube trains running does not bear thinking about. It would have been chaos. So the news that talks between the RMT union and London Underground had led to an amicable agreement were celebrated in this part of Surrey.

The planning to get to Wembley has not been as straightforward as I would have expected. Door to door from KT16 to HA9 is only about twenty miles but the number of choices for mode of transport on Sunday is quite bewildering. Car, train, tube, bus, boat, foot. Any combination of those. Whether the tube strike was on or off had a huge bearing on the intended route to take; but after an evening of surfing the Internet and looking at car parking possibilities, tube routes and train timetables (I lead such an exciting life) I finally have a plan.

A quick car journey to a tube station at the end of the Metropolitan line and then a few stops down to Wembley Park and a stroll along the Olympic Way to Wembley Stadium. Bob is your mother's brother.

Fever Pitch

This final planning for the trip on Sunday has heightened the sense of excitement. I thought that I was excited, but for Cardiff City fans the level of furore has reached fever pitch. Following the obvious anxious wait for tickets to land on the door mats of homes around the Welsh capital, or the five hour long queuing at the Ninian Park ticket office, the excitement levels amongst the Bluebirds' supporters have been escalating all week. Almost to a point of hysteria, I'm not sure if some will make it to the big day without bursting.

For Cardiff City fans, there is only one topic of conversation. What time to leave Cardiff? Which is the best route? Whether to stay over Saturday night or make a weekend of it? Where to meet before the game? Which shirt to wear - home blue or away black? And some more bizarre deliberations. Which socks to wear? What toast to eat on the morning of the game, brown bread or white? Or whether there has ever been a Cardiff streaker at Wembley? No doubt such matters of importance are also being discussed in South Yorkshire.

For me, I have the small matter of a Football League Two game at Wycombe Wanderers to take in on Saturday. A nice trip out into the Buckinghamshire countryside for a pub lunch and then down to Adams Park. That should keep my own feet on the ground ahead of the big one on Sunday. However, a colleague at work pointed out to me that I should, on a clear day, be able to see the Wembley arch from the high ground that surrounds Adams Park.

If that is the case, I can foresee only one outcome. I will probably faint.

Barnsley 0   Cardiff City 1
Semi-Final Sunday 6 April 2008
Attendance 82,752
Distance travelled 58 miles

"Men of Harlech on to glory
This will ever be your story
Keep these burning words before ye
Welshmen will not yield"

At the final whistle yesterday I witnessed scenes at a football game that I have not seen for a long, long time. A tide of emotion, jubilation, ecstasy, joy - words fail to express. Cardiff City had beaten Barnsley 1-0 to reach the FA Cup Final for the first time since 1927 and one half of Wembley erupted as referee Alan Wiley put the whistle to his lips. A mass of blue and white and a cacophony of celebration. Wembley's new foundations shook as over 33,000 danced like they've never danced before and sang like they've never sang before, belting out "Men of Harlech" that simply made the hairs stand up on the back of the neck. Grown men, women and children all around me were crying their eyes out. This was something quite magnificent. This was something I will never forget. I would be lying if I said there wasn't a tear in my eye nor a lump in my throat.

In stark contrast, the lonely figure of Kayode Odejayi stood head bowed framed only by the vastness of the Wembley pitch. The Barnsley striker had unwittingly provided one of the biggest talking points of the game when, clean through on goal and with only the Cardiff goalkeeper to beat, he contrived to miss the target. A guilt-edged chance that would have pulled the Yorkshire side level. At the final whistle Odejayi stood alone, fighting back tears of a different kind.

My day had started with a shock. Not the normal early morning shock when I look in the mirror, but the shock of opening the curtains to a winter wonderland picture postcard scene. A seriously large amount of the white stuff had dumped itself over Chertsey and snow several centimetres thick blanketed the ground. It took me a while for this to register. Hold on, snow on FA Cup Semi-Final day? It did not compute.

Game 15   Barnsley 0   Cardiff City 1

Shock soon turned to a small amount of concern. Would the game still be on? But then I snapped back to my senses and realised that this was the south of England. Snow down here only stays around for a couple of hours. No need to fret.

There were many highlights about the day yesterday. The ease of the journey for one. I picked up my road to Wembley mate PB and then drove to Hillingdon tube station and we were at Wembley Park before one could say "are we there yet?" A piece of cake. Also the fans. I couldn't believe how busy it was, arriving a full two hours before kick-off. It was a joy to walk down the Olympic Way and mingle with both Barnsley and Cardiff City fans. One could sense that both sets of supporters were out to make a day of it, no matter what. The losers of the game may not get the chance to play at Wembley again for a long time and the friendly, party mood atmosphere enhanced the occasion. I also met another road to Wembley bod, Timm Rutland, purely by chance as we strolled to the stadium. I had met Timm briefly at Middlesbrough and he made it to yesterday's game with his son. I hope they enjoyed the day as much as we did.

Although I have to say that the game itself was not brilliant. Sitting in with the Cardiff fans more than made up for it however. Wembley stadium is an impressive venue and the atmosphere and a fair degree of tension made the whole event highly absorbing and thoroughly entertaining, to the point that I felt quite drained by the time I arrived home.

Cardiff City had started the game as slight favourites. Barnsley had seen off Liverpool and Chelsea en route to the last four, but their League form is poor and they are currently involved in a relegation battle. Cardiff meanwhile have hit good form and have been playing some attractive football. All of which is, of course, totally irrelevant for a Wembley FA Cup Semi-Final.

Cardiff started in their trademark FA Cup fashion. An early goal, this time by Joe Ledley. Once again, it was a very good Cardiff goal. With

Game 15 Barnsley 0 Cardiff City 1

a mere nine minutes of play elapsed, a long throw from Capaldi into the box was half cleared for Ledley to strike a sweet volley over Luke Steele into the back of the net. It really was an impressive effort, Ledley almost steering the ball over a crowd of players. The Barnsley fans were stunned. The Cardiff fans went ballistic. Heart pounding stuff.

The first half then belonged to Barnsley in terms of possession. They responded better than Cardiff to the goal and won a series of corners that always provided an aerial threat. But the Cardiff back line held strong and it was impressive performances from Loovens and particularly Roger Johnson that thwarted the Barnsley offensive. Souza headed just wide from one of the corners and Brian Howard wasted a good chance. Odejayi also got in front of his marker only to shoot weakly at Enckelman in the Cardiff goal. Barnsley also had a shout for a penalty when Kevin McNaughton appeared to control the ball with his forearm as he shepherded the ball back to his keeper. Up at the other end Sinclair had a golden opportunity to nudge the ball past the advancing Luke Steele but Sinclair's first touch was too heavy; Steele did well to block the shot. Then back with Barnsley and the Hungarian Ferenczi headed just wide and soon after had a shot cleared off the line. All in all, Barnsley on top.

In the second half Cardiff started to control the game, putting their foot on the ball and making use of the Wembley space. The Cardiff midfield started to dominate and possession swung back to the team from Wales. Barnsley were now starting to visibly tire with the chase becoming more and more sapping. The experienced Hasselbaink began to influence proceedings, holding up play well thus allowing Whittingham, Rae and substitute Thompson to exploit some of the gaps that were starting to appear in all areas of the pitch. Rae had a great chance to close the game off on the hour mark when he met an excellent cross from Ledley but headed straight at the keeper.

Then on the 66th minute, the pivotal moment of the game. That miss from Odejayi. An uncharacteristic error from the Cardiff's centre back pairing

Game 15 Barnsley 0 Cardiff City 1

saw them step up too soon on the half way line and a through ball found Odejayi alone in acres of space in the Cardiff half. Bearing down on goal, with only Enckleman to beat, the equaliser seemed inevitable. It was a just a matter of waiting for the back of the net to ripple. But amazingly the striker, who has scored only one goal in twenty four games, pushed his shot wide. The Cardiff fans went wild, celebrating as one would celebrate a missed penalty, whilst the Barnsley fans to a man held their heads in utter disbelief.

Odejayi stood with his face buried in his hands. I know what it feels like to miss a sitter like that. I have absolutely no idea what it feels like to miss a sitter like that at Wembley in front of 33,000 expectant fans. Poor guy, football can be cruel at times.

One more long range effort from Whittingham and a chance for Rae to seal it when through on goal (but let down by a tired first touch) and that really was it. A case of Cardiff playing out time for the remainder of the game. The last twenty minutes went very slowly, Barnsley fans must have sensed that the game was now beyond them whilst the Cardiff fans had long since bitten off any remaining finger nails.

Then that final whistle, and those truly unbelievable scenes. Cue the hugs. Cue the tears. It was fitting that it was Joe Ledley, a local Cardiff lad, who had scored the only goal of the match. Aged only twenty one, welcome to the land of dreams.

This morning, I have had a little time to reflect. What a day. I really have run out of superlatives. This FA Cup run just gets better and better and better. There is no doubt in my mind that this remains football's greatest Cup competition. The English FA Cup. Yesterday it belonged to Wales and I feel extremely privileged to have been part of it all. I left Wembley yesterday with 'Men of Harlech' reverberating around the stadium, through the concourses and coursing through my body. I (and PB) hummed and whistled the tune all the way home. It is in my head still this morning.

Game 15 Barnsley 0 Cardiff City 1

Just one more game to complete the run. Back at Wembley on Saturday 17th May? Will I be there? Who can tell. The one certainty is that the 2007-08 FA Cup Final will be an all blue and white affair between Cardiff City and Portsmouth. Yes, you read that right. Cardiff City and Portsmouth. Quite unbelievable! The last two teams standing out of 731 teams. In that list of original entrants, Cardiff City were wedged in between Canvey Island and Carlisle United whilst Portsmouth sat snugly alongside Port Vale and Potters Bar Town.

In fact, all three of the Football Association's major Cup competitions have reached the Final stage. Before the weekend, the line-ups for the FA Vase Final and the FA Trophy Final were already decided: Kirkham & Wesham v Lowestoft Town and Ebbsfleet United v Torquay United respectively.

Sans Interdit

I found myself Saturday evening trying to explain to a stranger the complexities of qualification into European competition for clubs plying their trade in the English pyramid. The fact that the rather attractive brunette I was talking to had no interest whatsoever in football (I think she was a Tottenham fan) made the conversation somewhat perplexing. I couldn't even tell you how we arrived at that topic but she seemed genuinely interested. Or at least that's how I remember it.

It can be a confusing subject. How does one explain that the major European competition, the UEFA Champions League, is open to club sides who are not necessarily League champions? That an English team can finish as low as fourth in the Premiership yet still qualify for a competition so inappropriately named. Or that the winners of our two major English Cup competitions (the FA Cup and the League Cup, which is currently called the Carling Cup) gain entry to the UEFA Cup? At the same time trying not to confuse matters by dropping in the trivially useless fact that the UEFA Cup used to be called the Inter-Cities Fairs Cup and the winners of our Cup competitions used to qualify for a completely different competition called the European Cup Winners' Cup. But that doesn't exist anymore. Should one also mention that teams can also qualify for the UEFA Cup through League position? Add to that the scenario that either of our Cup winners may have already qualified for the Champions League and therefore a different team is offered entry into the UEFA Cup in their place. Not forgetting that there are also back-door routes into the UEFA Cup through the Intertoto Cup and the Fair Play League.

So many ifs and buts and permutations and possibilities. As clear as mud. It was a surprise that my party companion was still awake.

But I did have the sense to spare the girl any additional pain. One thing

Sans Interdit

I did not go anywhere near was an attempt to explain the situation that Cardiff City, who have reached this season's FA Cup Final, find themselves in. Should the Welsh club go on to win the FA Cup on May 17th, they would not be allowed to play in Europe next season. Their UEFA Cup entry would be taken by Portsmouth, their opponents at Wembley. I avoided this can of worms not only because I sensed that a state of narcolepsy was rapidly taking control of the young lady, but mainly because I still struggle to get my head around this issue myself.

In simple terms, the issue is something like this. Winners of the English FA Cup usually qualify for Europe but under current rules Cardiff City would not be allowed to as they are classed as a Welsh club. Even though Cardiff City play in the English pyramid, as a Welsh club they are not affiliated to the English Football Association (FA). As far as the FA are concerned, Cardiff City and other Welsh clubs play in England as 'guest' teams. England's representatives in European club competitions can only be FA affiliated English clubs.

In essence, Welsh clubs can only qualify for Europe through Welsh national competitions. To complicate matters UEFA rules stopped Cardiff City – as well as Swansea City, Wrexham, Colwyn Bay, Merthyr Tydfil and Newport County - from using Welsh competitions to reach Europe when they continued in the English League rather than join the League of Wales (now the Welsh Premier League) when it was first established.

The way things stand Cardiff City can never qualify for Europe. No entry. Or should I say "Sans Interdit".

UEFA may well now offer Cardiff City a lifeline; Michel Platini has gone on record as saying that UEFA would contemplate offering the club a 'wildcard' entry into next season's UEFA Cup should they beat Portsmouth next month. This would seem to offer a solution to keep all parties happy, but the Football Association of Wales (FAW) have balked at that particular suggestion. The FAW have long term plans to strengthen their own competitions, something that would only happen

Sans Interdit

if they could persuade the big Welsh clubs – such as Cardiff City – to play in them. Enticement to join the Welsh fold would be the carrot of European qualification offered through the Welsh Premier League. UEFA's wildcard proposal would undermine these long term FAW plans.

So this is an issue I'm sure we've not heard the last of. I sympathise with Cardiff City's plight and on the one hand I hope that common sense prevails, but on the other hand not if it serves to undermine the FAW's not unreasonable attempts to build a strong Welsh League. As for an amicable solution, there seems to be little light at the end of the tunnel.

In the meantime, the party brunette has suggested we meet for a Starbucks next week. She wants to hear my views on the offside rule. Of course I declined the offer. I'm a happily married man. And there's nothing trickier than trying to explain first phase football over a Café Mocha.

A Team Of (Mostly) Strikers

Jack Pitcher (Gloucester City), Matt Townley (Team Bath), Andy Forbes (Eastleigh), Craig Farrell (York City), Stuart Beavon (Weymouth), Craig Mackail-Smith (Peterborough United), Michael Mifsud (Coventry City), Alfie Potter (Havant & Waterlooville, on loan from Peterborough United), Luke Steele (Barnsley, on loan from West Bromwich Albion), Kayode Odejayi (Barnsley) and Joe Ledley (Cardiff City).

What do these eleven footballers have in common?

The answer? They will all be at Wembley for the FA Cup Final on May 17th. They are the Football Association's 'Team of the FA Cup' for 2007-08. Each player was voted as 'Player of the Round' by fans and receives a pair of VIP tickets for the Final, a trophy and £500 worth of football equipment for a local school of their choice.

The thing that strikes me about that list of names is that it does not include a single Premiership player. In previous seasons the team of the FA Cup has included the likes of Ruud van Nistelrooy, Shay Given, Luis Garcia, Steven Gerrard, Wayne Rooney, Frank Lampard and Jamie Carragher. But not one 'big name' this time around which must be quite unique. That fact alone goes some way to illustrating what an extraordinary competition it has been this season.

Most of the names will be unfamiliar to many. Jack Pitcher won the award for his First Qualifying Round performance; he scored all five goals in their 5-1 victory over Yate Town. The twenty four year old striker won 58% of the votes following the game in which he only had five chances, but netted them all.

It appears that if you had your scoring boots on in this season's FA Cup you had a better than most chance of picking up a 'Player of the Round'

A Team Of (Mostly) Strikers

award. Matt Townley scored a six-minute hat-trick for Team Bath in the 8-1 demolition of Moneyfields (yes, there really is a team called that). Andy Forbes scored three in Eastleigh's 5-0 win over Clevedon. York City's Craig Farrell scored an eight-minute hat-trick towards the end of their 6-0 victory over Rushall Olympic. Stuart Beavon scored a seven-minute hat-trick for Weymouth at Eastbourne Borough, a game attended by yours truly as part of this FA Cup venture.

Spot a trend? There's more. Peterborough United striker Craig Mackail-Smith claimed four goals in the 5-0 routing of Staines Town. Michael Mifsud netted a brace in Coventry City's excellent 4-1 victory at Blackburn in the Third Round and Alfie Potter scored for Havant & Waterlooville up at Liverpool. Potter is the only one to receive the award whilst playing for a team that exited in that round. Luke Steele in the Fifth Round is the only non-goalscorer after his brilliant performance between the sticks that helped Barnsley triumph at Liverpool. Goalscorers Kayode Odejayi (Barnsley) and Joe Ledley (Cardiff City) complete the line up. Bag a few goals and win a trip to Wembley!

No defenders or midfielders in the team and only one player who did not score a goal. As it is the fans who ultimately decide on the best player from each round, it shows what the fans value most and that is the ball thudding against the back of the onion bag. What that list also shows is what an inclusive competition the FA Cup is: the football clubs represented in the team of the tournament are scattered throughout all levels of the football pyramid. All the players selected have another thing in common: they have all gone on record as saying that they "love the FA Cup". Are you listening Dave Kitson?

What's more, I'm sure they'll love it even more once they are at the Final to witness the lifting of the famous old trophy. I doubt if Jack Pitcher, as he ran out for Gloucester City back in September last year, could have imagined that his season would have ended at Wembley. One question remains though; as Cardiff City's Joe Ledley will actually be playing on the big day, I wonder what will happen to his VIP tickets? I might give Joe a call.

Wembley At Chertsey

It seemed rather fitting somehow to go to the Chertsey Town v Wembley match, a Saturday afternoon Combined Counties League (Premier Division) encounter with a traditional 3pm kick-off. My FA Cup run had started here at this ground, Alwyns Lane, way back at the start of this season. A team called Wembley were in town for the final game of the campaign and catching this one felt quite apt.

The game had all the feel of a pre-season knock-about. Both teams have had a mediocre season and mid-table obscurity beckoned long before the Christmas lights had been taken down. Yesterday the sun was shining, the shorts and flip-flops were out in force and sun block was in order. Except the latter never crossed my mind and I ended up with a burnt bonce. My wife would later remark, with that kind of stifled amusement that is evident in a person who is impressed with their own quality of wit, that I resembled a bottle of tomato ketchup. Red with a white top. Thanks dear.

It certainly is relaxing going to a game when the venue is on your own doorstep. A lovely beer garden lunch (phase one of the forehead scalding) was followed by a quick peek at the closing ten minutes of the Chelsea - Manchester United game, including that late penalty that turned Sir Alex Ferguson's face the same colour as my head. Then a leisurely amble down to the ground, arriving a little after ten to three. A stampede to the (single) turnstile was never going to be an issue. I went to the game with old faithfuls PB and Mackem and fellow Chertsey resident Gee Jay.

The game itself was nothing to write home about, even if home was only around the corner. When Chertsey Town scored the only goal of the game the substitutes were still getting comfy in the dugouts. My watch still read 3pm, but I think the referee had either started the game a couple of minutes early or my watch was slow. A neat move saw the

Wembley At Chertsey

ball pushed out to the right and the resulting cross into the box was finished comprehensively. I'm not sure who scored for Chertsey. No tannoy announcements or big screen replays here. I'd like to say it was the number nine, John Pomroy, if only to get the chance to mention that he scored his 50th goal of the season last week. An impressive haul for any striker, irrespective of the standard of football. Law of averages dictates that it probably was Pomroy who slotted home.

Such an early goal always gives rise to thoughts of goal fests, but unfortunately for the crowd of 153, that was the end of the scoring. The pre-season ambience must have filtered through to both sides as neither showed any urgency in their play. Throughout the ninety minutes Chertsey Town were the more threatening and were the team in control. They had many chances to score, but just didn't seemed that bothered about doing so.

Inevitably, concentration on the lacklustre proceedings began to falter and my strongest memories are of peripheral goings on. These were, in the main, things that one is far more aware of at these smaller grounds, with the touchline only a few yards away. This is what I enjoyed so much in the earlier rounds of the FA Cup, being so close to the action that watching a game became a quite different experience altogether. The banter between players, the constant abuse of the referee and non-stop berating of the assistants. Big news this season has been the experimental efforts to minimise the stick that officials on the pitch receive, but it was interesting yesterday to hear the officials give as good as they got.

Particularly one of the referee's assistants. On one occasion, Wembley were defending a set piece. As the ball was centred, one of the Wembley centre backs stood with his arm raised high above his head (in Tony Adams fashion) and shouted "Oi! Lino! Offside!" The said defender was clearly the last man in the area, by a country mile. The assistant screamed back a response with some gusto "You're the one playing him on!!!" The only words missing at the end of his reply were "you plonker".

Wembley At Chertsey

As the game drifted on into the second half, we noticed that the Chertsey players were playing their own 'pass the coin' game. I have heard about this, but never witnessed it. The drill is something like this. One of the players (normally the captain) takes to the field with a small object, usually a coin, that can easily be transferred from player to player during the course of a game. There is a bet riding on which player is holding the coin at certain key points in the game, e.g. when a goal is scored. The player left in possession at such times would be the 'loser', and have to honour a bet, i.e. buy a round of drinks in the bar after the match. This was quite evidently happening, with the Chertsey full back Paul Bartholomew regularly receiving the coin. He spent most of the second half running around with his right hand clenched. No matter how often he relinquished the hot potato he seemed to get it back again. We lost track of the coin towards the end of the game, but my bet is that Bartholomew had an expensive evening.

Not a brilliant game then, but a comfortable three points for Chertsey Town to round off their season. A small group of young kids had started a game of football on a small area of grass just behind and below the terrace we were stood on, using a couple of Sainsbury's trolleys as one goal and a jumper and floodlight pylon as another. Frankly, their game was better. It ended 6-4. At the height of their contest, with the scores delicately balanced at 4-4, a wayward clearance flew in our direction. Yours truly nodded a fine goal in off a wobbly trolley wheel. To my dismay, one of the youngsters declared the goal null and void. He shouted up at me "that doesn't count" which I suppose was technically true. It was also at that point, as I headed the ball, that I realised how burnt my forehead was. Leather and third degree burning do not mix.

For Chertsey Town the curtain has drawn on another season. My season began at Chertsey with dreams of Wembley; Chertsey had ended theirs in the company of Wembley. In an almost poetic way, that deserves to be an end to any story. But for me, there is one chapter left. But before that final chapter, I just need to stick my head in a bucket of 'After Sun'.

The Final Countdown

There's an old saying that the more you watch the clock, the slower time passes. I seem to have been waiting an age for Saturday's FA Cup Final; six weeks will have elapsed between my last trip to Wembley and my next, but it feels much longer than that. When I was a kid, the six week summer holiday seemed like an eternity. This, by comparison, seems much longer. The slow passing of the minutes, hours and days is all the more painful with the knowledge I have one more game to take in. Only one more, the ultimate game. One final hurdle left before I can complete this gallop through the fourteen ties that have whittled 731 teams down to just two and, at its climax, to one eventual winner.

Should I worry that I might not complete this journey? I have surpassed all my own expectations. I envisaged getting as far as maybe the Fourth or Fifth Round before coming up against any number of insurmountable obstacles. I have already had one trip to Wembley. I now have a ticket for the Final on May 17th; it is up there on the shelf above my desk as I write. It rarely leaves my sight. I know that finally owning a golden ticket is a massive hurdle negotiated. I owe a friend so much.

I know I shouldn't watch time tick by, life is far too short, but there are still so many things that could go wrong in these final few days. I have had some near misses so far; my wife's volleyball injury (Dartford v Camberley Town) and my chest infection (Wolves v Cambridge United) being the most notable. Although I have that valuable ticket in my sweaty handed possession, other factors may yet prevent me from taking those last steps up Olympic Way.

Fire, pestilence, flood? Hardly. But one cannot rule out anything. I consider myself to have been extremely lucky so far the way this season's FA Cup has shaped up. No incredibly long journeys for me, no sight nor sound of a Premiership club until the Sixth Round Proper, no replays that clash

The Final Countdown

with any 'no you cannot get out of this' type of family occasion. Maybe it is time for my luck to run out?

A car breakdown? A tube strike? A blow to the head? A family crisis? A 'dog eats ticket' shock? I know I must put all those things to the back of my mind. But a kind of paranoia has started to take hold and once it starts it can only get worse.

Here's how my week looks.

Tomorrow I'm at the dentist. The possibilities for disaster are endless. A slipped drill creates a new cavity where there shouldn't be one. A malfunctioning chair rockets me up through the ceiling into the tanning salon above. I could be gassed by an incompetent anaesthetist. Patient records are mixed up at reception and I end up with full jaw brace and have to take on food through a straw for the foreseeable future. I could become another NHS blunder headline: "man has leg amputated in teeth cleaning fiasco". Gulp.

On Thursday I have a golf society day. A veritable minefield. A lightening strike on the first tee? A golf ball embedded in my temple or a stray tee embedded in my scrotum? I could step on a bunker rake and get smashed in the mush, cartoon style. I could shatter a kneecap as I attempt to break my clubs out of frustration. Not a safe environment.

Then on Friday, I take my son swimming. Where to start? A slip on a wet changing room floor to break a few bones? A momentary lapse in concentration as I forget to come up for air? A stumble off the diving board and a fall from a great height to wipe out the 'Aquarobics for Geriatrics' class. Or even a frenzied blood curdling shark attack? Perhaps not.

Good grief! The final countdown to the culmination of several months of effort should be a pleasurable period. But as the clock slowly ticks and tocks and tocks and ticks, I am working myself up into a state something

The Final Countdown

close to hysteria. If I'm this bad, just think what it must be like for the fans of, and everyone involved with, Cardiff City and Portsmouth. A hundred times worse I suggest.

If you are off to Wembley next Saturday, and I make it there in one piece, please do come over and say hello. You won't be able to miss me. I'll be the lummox wrapped in cotton wool.

The Innocence Of Youth

When my son opened the front door this morning, as we were rushing away for school, he was confronted by a huge cardboard box which had been left on the doorstep. In itself, quite exciting for an eight year old boy. The fact that this box carried my son's name on the address label was doubly exciting. The rush to school would simply have to be delayed for a little while yet.

Wide-eyed and fit to explode with excitement, my son tore at the box. I had no more of an idea what it contained that my son did, so I felt that same buzz, albeit dampened somewhat by age and years of experienced disappointments. But the innocence of youth is a marvellous thing to behold; for those few seconds, as the stubborn wrapping tape refused to be torn and the contents remained a secret, it was obvious that the youthful expectation was only of something good, great, wonderful. It was a huge cardboard box after all, how could he expect anything else?

Before the arrival of the box I had been looking through today's newspapers. I was keen to see how tomorrow's FA Cup Final was being covered by the national press. There is so much gripping football to be had at the moment, what with the Play-Offs, the FA Trophy and FA Vase Finals, the UEFA Cup Final involving Rangers and next week's game in Moscow. I feared that this season's FA Cup Final, with the big names absent, may be overshadowed somewhat by the all-English affair in the Champions League Final; I think to some extent this is true. But the game tomorrow is afforded some back page space.

Many newspapers are running the same story. It is about Cardiff City's exciting young prospect with the nickname of 'Rambo'.

Aaron Ramsey, in a quite charming way, displays all the innocence of youth. When Cardiff City arrive at Wembley tomorrow, Ramsey will

The Innocence Of Youth

be a mere 17 years and 144 days old. If Cardiff go on to win the Cup, he will replace Paul Allen's name in the record books as the youngest FA Cup winner in the history of the competition. His team mates hail him a "superstar in waiting". The Independent's headline today reads: "Wembley awaits Ramsey, the boy who would be king". No pressure then.

Last season Ramsey became Cardiff's youngest ever player, taking that crown from John Toshack. The prodigious young talent has already been courted by a host of Premiership clubs, with Sir Alex Ferguson allegedly leading the interest. The youngster from Caerphilly is seen by some as the natural successor to Paul Scholes up at Old Trafford. Ramsey has also been selected for the full Wales squad for their games against Iceland and the Netherlands later this month; and the Portsmouth camp, ahead of tomorrow's showpiece, have identified Ramsey as the real danger in the Bluebird's team. His playing style has been likened to that of Steven Gerrard.

It amazes me that for someone so young he does not appear to be fazed or hold any fear about tomorrow and is coping with the pressure that the attention and expectation bring. He could be playing in an FA Cup Final for heaven's sake, only a year after sitting his GCSEs.

There is an old Chinese proverb that says: "A new-born calf fears not the tiger". I just hope that Ramsey does not succumb to the nerves and the pressure that can come from playing in such a big occasion at Wembley. We have seen the occasion get to older, wiser, more experienced players in the past and has made the best players crumble under the burden. Ramsey would not be the first to be paralysed by the moment, and won't be the last.

But Ramsey seems to have a good head on his shoulders and in David Jones and other experienced players such as Hasselbaink and Fowler at Cardiff, he is well protected. His feet appear firmly secured. Following the Semi-Final, he is taking another Wembley appearance in his stride,

The Innocence Of Youth

but admits that he does not remember the old Wembley. He knows not of the twin towers. Now that makes me fell really old. Should I therefore be amazed that he holds no fear? How can one fear something never before experienced? Perhaps it is the total innocence of youth that will actually help and carry him through.

So Ramsey could write his name into the history books. To do this, tomorrow will be the day he will have to come of age, this child amongst men. He will have to remain calm and composed in a manner that will belie his age, and I'm sure he will. But if you look closely, very closely, you will undoubtedly get a glimpse of that wide-eyed excitement that can only ever be portrayed in the face of youth. I'm sure it will be there, just for a few fleeting seconds.

Just like my son opening that box this morning.

What was in the box? It was a radio-controlled football game won in a competition. A competition that he had entered in a kid's magazine. We had told him at the time that the chances of winning were slim at best. On the way to school he chatted excitedly about his win and carried a huge grin from ear to ear and all the way to the playground. He already has a plan for this evening. We will unpack the game, put the batteries in and play out a match. He has already decided that I will be Cardiff City and he will be Portsmouth.

He has already declared that he will thrash me. Ah, the innocence of youth.

Cardiff City 0 Portsmouth 1
Final Saturday 17 May 2008
Attendance 89,874
Distance travelled 58 miles

Waking up this morning I felt somewhat drained. Emotionally, mentally and physically. But in a satisfied and almost smug way. As my 16th FA Cup game drew to a close under the magnificent Wembley arch, the realisation of what I and my friends have achieved finally sunk in. In the whole scheme of things, it is something quite inconsequential. Especially so against the back-drop of cyclones, earthquakes, Third World poverty, the failing economy and melting ice caps. But for me, it has become a dream fulfilled. I am now nursing the morning after, and it all feels a bit surreal. Partly empty at the sudden conclusion of it all, but partly full to the brim with the wonderful memories I have collected, like keepsakes, along the way. Yesterday provided one last fantastic keepsake. If you have a moment, please let me tell you about my day.

The day was going to be all about the occasion. As with most Finals, a decent football game is a bonus. The game itself was far from classic, but intriguing nonetheless and one that was certainly entertaining. I awoke Saturday morning feeling very excited about the day, the culmination of my travels, but at the same time a little subdued. At first I thought this was due to the imminent closure of this little chapter of my life before I realised that was not the reason at all. I had already had one trip to Wembley, for the Semi-Final, and that was an unbelievable day. As I prepared to set off for my second visit in six weeks I was in an 'it can't be any better than the Semi-Final' state of mind.

Yet, not for the first time on this run, I was wrong. Going to an FA Cup Final is big. A first for me. I was not prepared for how much of a sense of occasion there is. Television coverage does not do it any justice at all. One cannot fail to be engulfed by it all, even as a neutral.

I was lucky and very pleased to be joined at the 2008 FA Cup Final at Wembley by two of my fellow journeymen, PB and Mackem. That and 89,871 significant others. The atmosphere in the Cardiff end of the stadium

Game 16   Cardiff City 0   Portsmouth 1

was, once again, quite electric. Add the noise reverberating around the stanchions from the Portsmouth end and the resultant mix was heady. Every seat in the house had a flag left beneath it - black and yellow for Cardiff, blue and white for Pompey - and the vista minutes before kick-off was a sea of flags waved. A sight and sound sensory overload.

When the teams emerged from the tunnel the decibel levels and excitement levels were cranked up several notches. Quite heart-stoppingly magnificent! With a huge spoonful of hindsight, the highlight of the occasion for Cardiff City was probably right there, right then. Cardiff City walking out for the 2008 FA Cup Final? Who'd have thought that? For the Premiership boys from Portsmouth, who were no doubt equally surprised to be there, the afternoon was to develop into something very, very special indeed.

It was Cardiff who started the stronger and enjoyed the majority of possession in the opening exchanges. They made the most of the wide Wembley pitch and played a high line that brought both full backs into play. Paul Parry and Jimmy Floyd Hasselbaink led the line for Cardiff but it was Joe Ledley who impressed the most early on. It was Ledley who played a delightful ball in to send Parry into a one-on-one with David James in the Portsmouth goal, but James smothered the effort from Parry on twelve minutes. For the first quarter, Cardiff were winning the second balls and quicker in midfield. For a team that has enjoyed early goals in their FA Cup run, that twelfth minute miss proved to be decisive.

Portsmouth slowly found their rhythm, and the on-field experience in the likes of James, Campbell, Mendes, Glen Johnson and Kanu began to show. Pompey also used the width of the pitch well and on more than one occasion delivered some telling crosses that tested an shaky looking Peter Enckleman in the Cardiff goal. On twenty one minutes, Portsmouth should have scored. Kanu did the hard part with some neat footwork that took him around Enckleman. With a chance that seemed easier to score, Kanu hit the post from six yards out. Cardiff City breathed a collective sigh of relief.

Game 16 Cardiff City 0 Portsmouth 1

The relief was short lived. Another good move from Portsmouth down the right resulted in a near post cross from Utaka. Encklemen's nervous start to the game was compounded as he fumbled the ball to Kanu who prodded home a simple effort.

Cardiff's response was almost instant. Paul Parry found space on the left and crossed deep to an on rushing McNaughton in space. He had to stretch for his shot and the result was never going to threaten the Portsmouth goal. A large section of the Cardiff support thought they had equalised a minute before the interval when Glen Loovens poked home, but the goal was disallowed for a clear handball in the build up.

The second half could have been billed the Sol Campbell show. Kanu, presumably for his goal, was given the official man-of-the-match award, but for me, it was Campbell in the heart of the Pompey defence who shone. He barely put a foot wrong. The Cardiff fans sat around me were starting to get slightly frustrated with their team's tactics. They often resorted to high balls into the box and Campbell won everything. The team from Wales enjoyed possession and battled hard on the fringes of the box, but just came up short at crucial times. One flag waving Cardiff fan yelled "it's just not enough" and he was spot on.

If Campbell failed to put a foot wrong, Hasselbaink by comparison couldn't keep his feet. I was disappointed with the Dutchman's display, who spent more time on the floor. He went down under challenges far too easily and looked to the referee far too often for help. There were numerous times when it would have been more advantageous to his team mates if he had stayed vertical.

Clear chances for either side were few and far between in the second forty five minutes. After fifty two minutes Kanu arrowed in a shot that was heading for the top corner before it hit Loovens' chest and out for a corner. A flurry of substitutions saw Whittingham replaced by Ramsey, Hasselbaink replaced by Thompson and Portsmouth took off Utaka and Mendes for Nugent and Diop respectively. Aaron Ramsey's entrance

Game 16 Cardiff City 0 Portsmouth 1

heralded more play on the deck for Cardiff, but not enough to break through the Portsmouth back line.

Cardiff City, as they pressed for the equaliser, were vulnerable to the counter-attack. Nugent forced Enckleman into a near post standing save from a crisp shot and Distin looked to be clear through on goal; a fine last ditch tackle from Roger Johnson stopped Distin in his tracks. Cardiff City had their fair share of corners and set pieces but it was that man Campbell who stamped his authority. A late, looping header from Loovens from a set piece drifted harmlessly over and with it Cardiff's last chance of salvaging something from the game.

And that was just about that. All the way through the game I felt that Portsmouth had just about the edge and in the end shaded it. Few were predicting an avalanche of goals and in the end it was an error that decided the outcome. Cardiff fell just that little short in quality, but made up for it in endeavour and desire. Portsmouth ended the day as winners of the 2008 FA Cup.

At the end of my second visit to Wembley this season, the final whistle celebrations were at the opposite end. The fans from Portsmouth in their blue and white lapped up the moment and deservedly so. The biggest cheer of the afternoon arrived as Harry Redknapp lifted the famous Cup aloft. A fitting personal climax to his season.

The Cardiff City fans stood dejected and tears of a different kind were wiped away. The majority stayed for the presentation of the trophy. No doubt a sad journey back down the M4, but I'm sure they are very proud of their club's achievement. So they should be. Despite the defeat, Cardiff City will treasure this FA Cup campaign.

And so, if it is memories we are talking about, then this season's FA Cup has provided them by the bucket load. In what has been an unforgettable competition, the magic of the FA Cup has been laid bare for all to see. Like a breath of fresh air, football fans of all ages, loyalties and persuasions

Game 16 Cardiff City 0 Portsmouth 1

around our island have been served up with an FA Cup competition that has been a joy to behold and will linger in the memory for many a season yet. For the fans of Cardiff City and Portsmouth, the memories will never fade. We may have to wait a long, long time before two clubs of the likes of yesterday's Finalists reach the last match again. My own recollections have been handsomely fed and watered as I have meandered through this season's tournament; I really am full to the brim and I don't think fate could have given me a better FA Cup season than this.

Here I am at the end of it all, full to bursting and emotionally and mentally drained. A road to Wembley completed. In my very first post, a full eight months ago, I invited you to "come on in, the water is lovely". I don't know about you, but I for one have had a simply unforgettable swim.

Only The Beginning

Can you see that question mark in the title of this, my first ever blog? Wick to Wembley? In my very first post I explained that the question mark was there for a reason, a very significant reason. It symbolised the fact that there was every chance that I would not complete this journey from Alwyns Lane, Chertsey to Wembley, North London. These two locations are physically separated by a mere 58 miles but I travelled 2,354 miles to get there.

The dust has now settled for me. I have deliberately let that be so before I came back to write this piece. All week I have thought that this last post would indeed be that. The last post. The final summary. A conclusion. The end. But in reality, it is only the beginning. And look, that there is no question mark this time in my post title, because this I know for sure.

When I say the dust has settled, that is not strictly true. There has been the odd whirlwind and eddy of activity since last Saturday. For a couple of days (Monday was the worst on my return to work) I felt quite down. Quite hollow, as if something had been taken from me. This FA Cup adventure has played a significant part in my life for eight months and it ended as suddenly and as quickly as it had started. A few days in to the week and the expected newspaper and radio interviews came and went. Many, many messages of congratulations were received; thanks to everyone who made the effort to contact me. This whole FA Cup thing has remained high on my agenda.

In the middle of the week we were served up the "game of all games", the Champions League Final between Chelsea and eventual winners Manchester United. Probably over-billed, but a very good game with a dramatic end. But the thing that struck me most at the end was, within minutes, with the trophy barely lifted, thoughts back in the studio and with the players on the pitch turned to next season. What would happen

Only The Beginning

to Avram Grant? Would Chelsea sell most of their players? Is this start of a period of dominance from the Reds from Manchester? Ronaldo - staying or going?

Football never stands still. There really is no end. Many clubs are already deep into planning, scheming and plotting about next season whilst this season has not truly finished. Promoted clubs gear up for life at a higher, tougher level. Relegated clubs have already come to terms with their fate and are adjusting accordingly. In the lower levels of the non League pyramid decisions have already been made (and don't forget it is still only May) about League restructuring; some clubs already know which League they will be playing in following enforced sideways moves based on geographical location and changing League numbers. In football the dust is never allowed to rest.

With me the same is kind of true. I am now entering a period where I have some tough decisions to make. I am mulling over a serious book offer - who would have though that back in August? - and it is a decision I cannot afford to take lightly. I have rediscovered my taste for writing and I hunger for more. This blog, and more specifically the response to it, has been a real eye-opener. This is indeed the last post for this particular site, but I have a feeling another blog may be just around the corner. But who knows? Let me think on it for a while.

And what of the FA Cup? The journey for me was more important than the end. I have not been surprised with what I have found. The FA Cup is alive and well and it is not only about the big boys. Far from it. It is about clubs and teams from all over our land, in the villages and small towns and local communities. You or I could play in the FA Cup; I know some of you reading this have. On heavy pitches surrounded by single railings on miserably wet October days in front of fifty people. Knowing that game could be the first steps on a footpath that grows into a magnificent road, a road that leads all the way to Wembley.

I have already found myself wistfully looking through the list of teams

Only The Beginning

who have requested to be in the 2008-09 FA Cup. Some will not be accepted, but some new first-timers will. The list is made up of names such as AFC Wulfrunians, Heather St John and Walsall Wood. A world away from 2007-08 winners Portsmouth but undoubtedly still part of the same FA Cup family. The draw for the next season's Extra Preliminary Round will be made in only a few weeks time.

I wonder who Chertsey Town will draw. Wick again? Who knows? This is the beauty of the FA Cup. Only a matter of weeks and we will be back at the start. Return to go. For me, I know I have not reached an end, but arrived at the beginning. Of that, there is no question.

The Season's End

The FA Cup Finalists Cardiff City and Portsmouth played out their League campaigns, with one eye on their sojourn to Wembley, at a time when many teams across the country had already reached their season end. But how have the teams I have encountered in this FA Cup faired in the 2007-08 season? As one would expect, there has been a mix of fortunes.

Mid-table respectability (or mid-table obscurity, depending on the ambitions or expectations at the start of the season) was the final resting place for a few of the clubs. I have **Chertsey Town's** campaign and their 1-0 win over Wembley on the last day lifted them into the upper half of the table. They ended up playing three games in the FA Cup and in the FA Vase they were out by September after a 5-1 reverse against Deal Town. Another club that I visited for an FA Cup tie from the same League (Combined Counties Premier Division) were **Camberley Town** who had a far more successful season with a 3rd place League finish, six games in the FA Cup and a successful run in the FA Vase, reaching the Fifth Round before succumbing to Concord Rangers.

The middle reaches of the table were also final resting places for **Sittingbourne** and **Bromley**. Sittingbourne, who eliminated Chertsey Town in early September, finished 9th in Ryman Division One South, a League won by fellow Kent outfit, Dover Athletic. The FA Trophy wasn't any kinder for them, losing in October in the First Qualifying Round to Northwood. Bromley had a tense culmination to their Blue Square South season. For a long time just outside the promotion chasing pack (aiming for the Blue Square Premier) they still had a mathematical chance of sneaking into the Play-Offs. However, a last day home defeat quashed any dreams and Bromley ended up down in 11th, missing out by only five points in what was a very tight top half of the table.

The Season's End

For **Weymouth**, their run-in to the end of the season was equally tense, but not in the way they would have hoped. For a long time embroiled in a Blue Square Premier relegation battle, they escaped with an 18th place finish, five points above the drop zone. Their defeat at Cambridge United in December was their fourth FA Cup game. In the FA Trophy they lost in the Third Round to eventual Finalists Ebbsfleet United.

Wolverhampton Wanderers have been typically inconsistent this season and missed out on a Championship Play-Off appearance on goal difference despite a last day 1-0 home victory over Plymouth Argyle. Wolves finished 7th in an incredibly tight League; West Bromwich Albion took the title and with it promotion, to be joined by Stoke City and Hull City. I witnessed all three of Wolves' FA Cup games, culminating in that defeat at Cardiff City.

The Blue Square South side **Eastbourne Borough** finished runners-up to local rivals Lewes. The men from Priory Lane led the League for a large chunk of the season, but could not hold on to their position in the final stretch, winning only one of the last six games. Consigned to the lottery of the Play-Offs, the Sussex side cruised passed Braintree Town to book a place in the Final against Hampton & Richmond Borough. Eastbourne won 2-0 with late goals from Nathan Crabb and Paul Armstrong. The successful climax to the season ensures that the part-time club will be playing Blue Square Premier League football next season.

Cambridge United finished 2nd in their League, behind Blue Square Premier runaway leaders Aldershot Town. The club enjoyed five FA Cup games but lost in the FA Trophy in January to local rivals Histon. Another of our teams to reach the Play-Offs, they knocked out Burton Albion 4-3 on aggregate in the Semi-Final before the heartbreak of a Play-Off Final defeat at Wembley, going down 1-0 to Exeter City.

But out of all the teams I've seen the most successful club has to be **Dartford** who were crowned League champions a few weeks before the end of the season. They won the Ryman Division One North by nine points, losing only seven games. The team I have watched most in this season's FA Cup, they scored an impressive 107 League goals, 31 one of them coming from the division's leading scorer Brendon Cass. Dartford have swept most teams aside with apparent ease this season, chalking up some impressive score lines; 7-2 v Witham Town, 6-1 v Enfield Town, 6-1 v Canvey Island and three separate 5-0 wins. And their supporters have turned out in force, averaging 1,135 at Princes Park. To put that figure in context, the next best average was Canvey Island's 325. Congratulations to Dartford.

It goes without saying that for both **Cardiff City** and **Portsmouth** the FA Cup provided the culmination of a memorable season. The team from Wales finished mid-table in the Championship whilst Pompey ended their campaign in 8th position, their highest ever finish. But the FA Cup campaign including two Wembley appearances allows both clubs and sets of supporters the right to lay claim to a successful 2007-08. Following Portsmouth's lifting of the famous trophy, they will now compete in Europe for the first time in their history.

And what of **Wick**, the club who gave its name to the blog and book title? Playing in the Sussex County League Division One, they finished a credible 5th, with Crowborough Athletic winning the title. Wick fell at that first hurdle in the FA Cup against Chertsey Town; in the FA Vase they stayed in the competition until October before losing to fellow Sussex outfit Ringmer, losing 2-0 in the First Round Proper.

And finally, as I write this, the draw for the FA Cup 2008-09 competition has already been made. I couldn't help perusing the fixtures to see who Chertsey Town and Wick have drawn. Wick start in August with a home tie against Molesey, one of my local teams. Chertsey also have a home draw against Deal Town (from Kent), and if they win that they travel to Sittingbourne.

Now, does that fixture ring any bells?

Epilogue

In the few days following the FA Cup Final I wrote that this whole journey had been a quite memorable experience for me, memories that will stay with me forever. A couple of months on and those sentiments remain.

When I started this back in August, on a whim, I no had no idea what to expect. I was already besotted by the competition yet at the same time rather saddened by its perceived demise. In an era where we are saturated with live football through a raft of mediums, many of which seemed totally unimaginable twenty, fifteen or even ten years ago – I still marvel at the fact that watching a match on a laptop is something quite normal – the FA Cup has had a tough battle to remain in the hearts and minds of spoilt football fans.

To be honest I was confident in what I would find. I knew that the FA Cup still appeals, to clubs and fans alike. And I knew that the competition continues to present to us some quite incredible moments, 'hairs standing up on the back of the neck' kind of moments. This season, one only has to think of Chasetown, Horsham, Staines Town, Havant & Waterlooville, Oldham and Barnsley. True, the competition still has its detractors, and will continue to. But one senses that these are in the main the types of supporters who are bloated on Champions League style viewing, comfortable in their armchairs or kicking back in their padded box seats at games, enjoying a five course meal at half-time and back out to their exclusive balcony to watch the last ten minutes of the game.

The 2007-08 FA Cup was an exceptional competition as all the big teams stumbled, stuttered and eventually fell by the wayside. Fate had once again been kind to me, and I still pinch myself at the fortune of being part of it all. In the fight to convince authorities and fans alike that the FA Cup continues to hold a significant position in the ethos of British

Epilogue

football, the FA Cup this season won a major battle.

But for as much as I thought I knew, I learned so much more in spades. The FA Cup took me back to what I would call 'real' football, in the lower echelons of the game. The non League world that for the majority is out of sight and quite often out of mind. The small clubs, the crumbling grounds, the sloping pitches. I was presented with games where you didn't have to sit, wedged into a confined space for ninety minutes, where you could wander around all sides of the ground. Games without segregation where opposing supporters mix freely, trade banter and share views. Matches where you could talk to the players without fear of being jumped on by a yellow mass of security guards.

But for me the biggest memory I have is of the people I have met and talked to from all parts of the country, all walks of life and from clubs at all levels. There are men and women the length and breadth of the country that dedicate their time to their local club. They are the life blood of the clubs and by association, the life blood of football. The club committees, the club secretaries, the ladies and gents running club shops, the programme sellers, turnstile operators, groundsmen and tannoy announcers. The hard working managers of message boards and fans forums, websites and supporters clubs. All devoted and enthusiastic individuals upon whom the game of football relies. The unsung heroes.

At a time when the mass media concentrates on the darker side of football; greedy players, selfish agents, money-grabbing owners, the newspaper-selling headlines could not be anymore misleading. The football family is made up of honest, reliable, extremely hardworking and genuinely nice human beings. Everyone I met on my road to Wembley can be described thus. Football is not a game of ninety minutes. It is much, much more. And to those of you I have met that makes this so, you have made my FA Cup journey what it ended up being; a totally unforgettable and at times quite emotional experience.

And for that I am most grateful.

afrikids

AfriKids is a grass roots child rights Non Governmental Organisation working with families in northern Ghana to improve life for their most vulnerable and disadvantaged children. Our philosophy is to:

Listen to what a community knows it needs
Empower them to make the necessary changes themselves
Ensure absolute accountability and sustainability

£1 from the sale of this book will go to fund AfriKids' incredible work. To read more about AfriKids visit www.afrikids.org

Thank You